The Barrymores

The Barrymores

HOLLYWOOD'S FIRST FAMILY

Carol Stein Hoffman

THE UNIVERSITY PRESS OF KENTUCKY

Publication of this volume was made possible in part by a grant
from the National Endowment for the Humanities.

Published by The University Press of Kentucky
Scholarly publisher for the Commonwealth,
serving Bellarmine University, Berea College, Centre
College of Kentucky, Eastern Kentucky University,
The Filson Historical Society, Georgetown College,
Kentucky Historical Society, Kentucky State University,
Morehead State University, Murray State University,
Northern Kentucky University, Transylvania University,
University of Kentucky, University of Louisville,
and Western Kentucky University.

Editorial and Sales Offices: The University Press of Kentucky
663 South Limestone Street, Lexington, Kentucky 40508–4008

05 04 03 02 01 5 4 3 2 1

All illustrations, unless otherwise indicated, are from the collection of John Drew Barrymore.
Endpaper: Book plate designed and rendered by John Barrymore Sr.
Frontispiece: Portrait of John Barrymore and Dolores Costello Barrymore, 1928.

Library of Congress Cataloging-in-Publication Data

Hoffman, Carol Stein, 1937-
The Barrymores : Hollywood's first family / Carol Stein Hoffman.
p. cm.
Includes bibliographical references and index.
ISBN 0-8131-2213-9 (cloth : alk. paper)
1. Barrymore family. 2. Actors—United States—Biography. I. Title.
PN2285 .H59 2001
791.43'028'092273—dc21

2001003035

∞ This book is printed on acid-free paper meeting
the requirements of the American National Standard
for Permanence in Paper for Printed Library Materials.

Manufactured in South Korea.

Design by Stephanie Foley

John Drew Barrymore, Ralph Anthony Lumi,

and Carol Stein Hoffman

wish to dedicate this endeavor to their parents,

John Barrymore and Dolores Costello Barrymore,

Catherine Malaspino Lumi, and

Marion and Leon Stein

with love

Contents

Foreword

BY LEONARD MALTIN

I FIRST FELL UNDER THE SPELL of John Barrymore when I was in my early teens and read Gene Fowler's colorful biography *Good Night, Sweet Prince* for the first time. I'd fallen in love with films of the 1920s and 30s by then and even set my alarm to wake up in the middle of the night to see *Twentieth Century* the first time it was shown on television. For weeks to come, I would try to imitate the sonorous voice of John Barrymore intoning the words, "I close the iron door on you!" to his long-suffering minions.

One of my mentors was a wonderful actor named John Griggs, who had an extraordinary 16mm film collection and was eager to share it with young, impressionable people. (Among his other protégés were film scholar and preservationist David Shepard and actor Peter Coyote.) A longtime member of the Players Club in New York City, housed in the former residence of Edwin Booth on Gramercy Square, Griggs was a man of the theater, and a Barrymore devotee. I suppose I caught the bug from him; I've never gotten over it.

John Barrymore and his extraordinary family remain a source of endless fascination to me (and many others as well). The idea that one of the twentieth century's greatest actors was a reluctant thespian and that his equally celebrated brother would have been content to paint and compose music is all part of the mystique.

Reading about their forebears is interesting, too, even though we are forced to make do with second- and third-hand accounts of their work on stage, while John, Lionel, and Ethel still live on in the many films they made.

Every time I think I know all there is to know about the Barrymores (and the Drews and Costellos) I learn something new. Many of those nuggets have come from Carol Hoffman, who over the past decade has shared many of her discoveries with my wife Alice and me. We'll never forget the night Carol and her husband Ralph Lumi brought over one of John and Dolores Costello's meticulously maintained, oversized scrapbooks. To run our hands across those pages, examine private photographs from their honeymoon trip to the Galapagos Islands, read congratulations notices for the birth of their first child was positively thrilling.

It is that same sense of discovery—on a personal, first-hand level—that makes this book so rewarding. I defy anyone to read Carol's introductory chapter about meeting John Drew Barrymore and deciding to help him preserve his family's mementoes, and not be eager to learn the whole story.

Even familiar passages of the Barrymore saga have new life in this telling, because of the unique material Carol was able to draw upon. The many rare, striking, and often revealing photographs speak for themselves.

There aren't many names from the history of American theater that still strike a resounding chord today. Thanks to the still-blossoming career of a talented young woman named Drew, the Barrymore name still has meaning in the era of MTV.

I know this book will please the many admirers who still worship at the Barrymore shrine. I hope it will also serve as an introduction to a new generation, and perhaps inspire them to seek out the work of Drew's grandparents on film. No author—or granddaughter—could ask for more.

Preface

ONE DAY IN LATE WINTER 1981, after visiting an inventor friend and his wife at the Park Sunset Hotel, my fiancé and I stood in the hall outside their apartment saying our good-byes. Ralph turned and spotted a distinctive figure ducking into an apartment down the hall.

"John?" Ralph called. "John Barrymore?"

"No!" the man shouted as he darted into his doorway. In a moment, his head popped out again. "Is it YOU?" he asked as he squinted in Ralph's direction.

My friend and companion, Ralph Anthony Lumi, has been a trusted friend of the Barrymore family for more than thirty-five years. Recognition dawned on John's face, and without further hesitation we were invited in.

John Drew Barrymore was in his late forties when I met him. He was lean and muscular, and he moved with a grace that made me think of a gymnast. His stance was seaworthy, feet planted wide and solid as though he stood on a rolling deck. His nearly white hair and full beard made him seem much older than his years.

At this time John was doing some writing. Joe Loesy said that his screenplay about Billy the Kid was the best treatment that he'd ever seen on the topic. John's son, Johnny, leased the apartment next door to him. John's mother, Dolores Costello Barrymore, had recently died. Her estate was in probate and the family was in disarray. Not too long after our first meeting John moved from the Park Sunset to the Casa Royale, where he had room to house a large portion of his mother's materials.

The Casa was on Harper just south of Sunset. John's apartment was on the first floor at the end of a hallway.

A little beyond his front door, a window overlooked a patio. In front of the window, John had created a small altar covered with pieces of fresh fruit and bits of Meissen porcelain, remnants of days of splendor, leftovers from the estate his father had purchased from King Vidor in the days of the great movie moguls, back when movie stars did not pay income taxes and lived like royalty in the sun. The house had been the honeymoon home of John's parents, filled with treasures from the Galapagos Islands, Alaska, Guatemala, and Ecuador. John was born into its splendor but had lived there only his first four years; clearly there was a longing in his soul for those innocent days.

A low wooden chest sat in the small entryway of John's Hollywood apartment. On the top of the chest he had arranged a few treasures. One was a post-production shot from *When a Man Loves*. The photo shows the crew standing behind the seated actors, who are dressed in full period costume. John's father slouches in the center of the photo, a short cigarette between his fingers, looking directly at the camera, managing to appear very masculine in his brocades and slippers and tights. To his left, John's angelic mother, with her halo of bright hair and her shapely bare shoulders, leans slightly toward the camera but stares into the distance with a half smile.

The living room was a conglomeration of treasures juxtaposed with John's necessities. Lying on the floor was a folio of original Hogarth lithographs. A Travertine marble-topped Louis Quinze chest with two hand-painted panels in the style of Boucher stood in the corner. John's father's desk was the most prominent piece of furniture in the small living room. Above it hung a portrait of John as a small boy.

Cast and crew of *When a Man Loves* (1927); Jack Barrymore and Dolores Costello Barrymore are seated in the center of the front row. John Drew Barrymore has always liked this photograph of his parents.

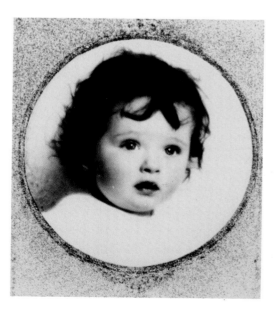

Portrait of John Drew Barrymore
as a child, circa 1934.

I remember watching John, seated behind that desk, holding daughter Drew on his lap, his white head bent over her golden one, listening to the tales she had to tell.

John's bedroom was at the end of the hall, but because the building's elevator created a disturbance there, he slept in the living room. Dolores Costello's materials resided in a large open closet that was more of a puzzle than an assistance. Two dressers stood in a corner at right angles and couldn't be opened at the same time. A small vanity table held precarious stacks of boxes. Some of the materials were neatly arranged and others were strewn and neglected. Mice had already digested portions of the treasures while they were stored in the old barn of the Dolores's avocado ranch in Fallbrook, California, and time was bestowing no gifts on the remainder.

JOHN MADE MANY overtures to us, subtly suggesting that we might get involved in a project with him and the Barrymore/Costello material. Ralph and I avoided the issue each time it arose. As an artist, I thought I knew what a monumental task cataloging the mass of materials would be, though as it turned out I had no real idea. But John was living in a cramped combination of library and museum—a little like a family mausoleum. He felt an obligation to preserve his family history, but he had no idea how that could be accomplished. Finally one day when he implored us for help in a most theatrical shriek, we could no longer deny him.

We discussed what sort of arrangement would most benefit all of us, should any benefits materialize from our collaboration. John suggested a solution. "Forget the lawyers," he said. "We'll do this under the ancient laws of USUFRUCT." In civil law, he told us, USUFRUCT is the right of enjoying a thing that belongs to another, drawing from the thing all of the profit, utility, and advantage that it may produce, provided that the substance of the thing remains unaltered. So, we entered the adventure together, all of us agreeing to John's definition but little realizing what we had signed on for or that the process would take over twenty years.

"Read everything," John said. And, of course, there was no other way to begin.

THE CASA ROYALE was the perfect setting for our discovery of old Hollywood. The three-story Spanish-Moorish structure had a wide staircase abutted by massive steps and flanked by large blue ceramic vases. A small white wrought iron balcony stood over the entry. Under the building was the garage, from which carbon monoxide fumes escaped and wafted faintly up the elevator and into the Barrymore Project office, which was John's noisy, crowded back bedroom. We worked there for many months until one day there was no money to pay the rent and it was time to move.

John moved in with a friend, a one-eyed Carpathian who lived on Curson below Sunset. We took a great portion of what was now called the Barrymorebelia home with us to Atascadero, California. Finally the collection could be stored and worked on in one place.

During this period John was feuding with the banks, accusing financial managers of looting the family treasures and selling them to insiders for a pittance. The probate of his mother's estate continued, family relationships pushed and tugged at him, and he raised funds by pawning family heirlooms with friends and in some cases trying but failing to keep thieves at arm's length. Soon John and his visually challenged host had a parting of the ways, and some of the "booty" had to be forcibly retrieved.

Don Behrstock offered us the use of his house above Sunset off La Cienega, and we jumped at the offer. Soon the empty house contained our sleeping bags and evidence of Barrymores past. John moved in with us, and with him right there to identify each item and describe its background, the work moved swiftly. When we returned to Atascadero, he stayed on at the Miller Drive house.

What we began in 1983 has since become a collated, filed, cross-referenced, historically sequenced work in progress. The families' personal letters and diaries describe life on the stage and in film from its birth through the transition to sound to the days when Hollywood stars were America's gods and goddesses. Letters, diaries, and articles from contemporary publications illuminate the large body of photographic material. Two Moroccan leather–bound albums embossed with the Barrymore crest contain complete sets of stills from Warner's *Sea Beast* and *When a Man Loves.* Jack and Dolores Costello Barrymore's honeymoon album was shot in the Galapagos Islands and Ecuador in 1928 and 1929. Dolores saved her two baby albums and her own correspondence and memorabilia as well as that of her husband, Jack Barrymore; her father, Maurice Costello, Vitagraph's first movie star; her mother, Mae Costello, her manager and friend; and her sister, actress Helene Costello.

The Great Barrymores—Lionel, Ethel, and Jack—whose names were a guaranteed draw for theatergoers and patrons of moving pictures for many years, were the offspring of actors. When Jack married Dolores Costello, he joined the mighty Barrymore bloodline to that of yet another performing family of stage and screen. The history of these lines encompasses the history of theater and film and is valuable for that reason, but the appeal of the individuals—the Flying Barrymores, the Royal Family of Hollywood, the Great Profile, the Man with the Dimples, the Goddess of the Silver Screen—makes the history fascinating.

Anyone who had an encounter with one of the legendary Barrymores was bound to repeat the tale, for brushing up against America's handsomest man or funniest woman or most talented character actor meant at least a small amount of adventure. Nearly every Hollywood autobiography of the past one hundred years mentions at least one member of the family; consequently, we are left with myriad comments by thousands of luminaries of Hollywood—as well as an untold number of descriptions of Barrymores about Barrymores, and Drews about Drews, and Drews about Barrymores, and so on—which have now become the legends of Broadway and Hollywood.

Acknowledgments

CAROL STEIN HOFFMAN, RALPH ANTHONY LUMI, AND JOHN DREW BARRYMORE have explored this project together and contributed to it equally, though in different ways. The work took us many places, and we were counseled and encouraged by helpful, knowledgeable people to whom we will be eternally grateful. They include John Blyth Barrymore, Tony Barrymore, who offered to aid us in any way he could and who made negatives of his grandparents' albums for us to use, Drew Barrymore, Diedre Le Blanc, John Drew Miglietta, Carol Vogel, Suezan Pierce, John Desco, Beverly Coburn, Richard Alcala, Nicole (Ferris) Scott, Mike Ferris, Michael Greene, Peter Maier, Frank Mazzola, Joe Valeno, Victoria Reiter, Rosalie Muskatt, Hiedi Kieserman, William Randolph Hearst Jr., Rayenna Martin, Bob Pavlik, Nancy Lowe, Judy Altman, Melody Coe, Mary Corliss, Donald Albrecht, Dr. Robert Henderson, Lois and Dave Berman, Barbara and Al Lyons, Marion Chaite Howe, Phyliss Freeman, Joe Rameriz, Dale McFann, Philip Rhodes, Daniel Culliton, Patrick Culliton, Ed Sievers, Mike Downey, Roger Montgomery, Sarah Dorfman, Al Matthews, Colonel Bigler, Bruce Petty, Bruce Grakal, Bob Lilley, Don Behrstock, Larry Minor, Nicole Miner, Sheila Horowitz, Gary Horowitx, Lee Everett and Bill Shluder, Tim Englert, Ken Wlaschin, Tony Slide, Leonard and Alice Maltin, David Mumford, Bruce Gorden, Stephanie Savage, Howard Prouty, Ellen Harrington, Wendy Hoffman, Greg Hoffman, Lorraine Hoffman, Issac Hoffman, Camille Hoffman and Lauran Hoffman.

Louisa Lane Drew (1820–1897): daughter of Thomas Frederick Lane and Eliza Trenter Lane; step daughter to John Kinlock; half sister to Adine Kinlock and Georgiana Kinlock; wife of Henry Hunt Blaine, George Mossop, and John Drew Sr.; mother of Wisa Drew, Jack Drew, and Georgie Drew

John Drew Sr. (1827–1862): son of Mr. ? Drew, treasurer of Niblo's Theatre in New York; brother of Edward Drew, Frank Drew, and George Drew; husband of Louisa Lane; father of Wisa Drew, Jack Drew, and Georgie Drew, and possibly Adine Stephens ("Aunt Tibby")

John ("Jack") Drew Jr. (1853–1927): son of John Drew and Louisa Lane Drew; brother of Wisa Drew and Georgie Drew; husband of Josephine Baker; father of Louisa Alexia ("Bee") Drew

Georgiana ("Georgie") Emma Drew Barrymore (1855–1893): daughter of John Drew Sr. and Louisa Lane Drew; wife of Maurice Barrymore; mother of Lionel Barrymore, Ethel Barrymore, and Jack Barrymore

Sidney White Drew ("Uncle Googan") (1863?–1919): adopted son of Louisa Lane Drew; possibly the natural son of John White and Maria Drew White; adopted brother of Wisa Drew, Jack Drew, and Georgie Drew; husband of Gladys Rankin and Lucille McVey; father of Sidney Rankin Drew

Maurice Herbert Blyth ("Barry") Barrymore (1847–1905): son of William Edward Blyth and Charlotte Matilda de Tankerville Chamberlayne; brother to William Blyth; husband of Georgie Drew Barrymore; father of Lionel Barrymore, Ethel Barrymore, and Jack Barrymore

Lionel Herbert Barrymore (1847–1954): son of Maurice Barrymore and Georgie Drew Barrymore; brother of Ethel Barrymore and Jack Barrymore; husband of Doris Rankin and Irene Fenwick; father of Mary Barrymore and Ethel Barrymore

Ethel Mae Blyth Barrymore Colt (1879–1959): daughter of Maurice Barrymore and Georgie Drew Barrymore; sister of Lionel Barrymore and Jack Barrymore; wife of Russell Colt; mother of Samuel Colt, Ethel Colt, and Jackie Colt

John ("Jack") Sidney Blyth Barrymore (1882–1942): son of Maurice Barrymore and Georgie Drew Barrymore; brother of Lionel Barrymore and Ethel Barrymore; husband of Katherine Corri Harris Barrymore, Blanche Oelrichs (poet Michael Strange), Dolores Costello Barrymore, and Elaine Jacobs (Barrie) Barrymore; father of Diana Blanche Blyth Barrymore, Dolores Ethel Mae "Dede" Barrymore, and John (Blyth) Drew Barrymore

Dolores Costello Barrymore (1903–1979): daughter of Maurice G. Costello and Mae Altschuh Costello; sister to Helene Costello; wife of Jack Barrymore and Dr. John Vruwink; mother of Dede Barrymore and John Drew Barrymore

Diana Blanche Blyth Barrymore (1920–1960): daughter of Jack Barrymore and Blanche Oelrichs (poet Michael Strange); half sister to Dede Barrymore and John Drew Barrymore; wife of Bramwell Fletcher, John Howard, and Robert Wilcox

John Drew Barrymore (1932–): son of Jack Barrymore and Dolores Costello Barrymore; brother to Dede Barrymore; half brother to Diana Barrymore; husband of Cara Williams, Gabriella Palazzoli, and Ildiko Jaid Mako Barrymore; father of John Blyth Barrymore, Blyth Barrymore, and Drew Barrymore

John Blyth Barrymore (1954-): son of John Drew Barrymore and Cara Williams; half brother to Drew Barrymore; husband of Rebecca Pogrow; father of John Barrymore IV, Blyth Barrymore, and Sabrina Barrymore

Antony John Barrymore Fairbanks (1952–): son of Dede Barrymore Fairbanks and Thomas Fairbanks

Drew Barrymore (1975–): daughter of John Drew Barrymore and Ildiko Jaid Mako Barrymore; half sister to John Blyth Barrymore; wife of Jeremy Thomas and Tom Green

And a cast of thousands

The Lanes

Thomas Haycroft Lane ——— Louisa Rouse

Thomas Frederick Lane ——— Eliza Trenter
1796-1825   1796-1887

1 Henry Blaine Hunt
1796-1854

2 George Mossop
1814-1849

Louisa Lane ——— 3 John Drew
1820-1897   1827-1862

The Lanes

And perhaps the fact of four generations of this same family having engaged in the profession of acting—with credit to their calling, and honor to themselves–may still further emphasize the real worth of that calling, both to the individuals engaged therein and the world at large.

—JOHN DREW JR.

Though details are lost in time, the Lane family line of actors and managers stretches back to players strolling at the time of Elizabeth I. "For the record," wrote Lionel Barrymore, "the necrologists and genealogists have unearthed dusty playbills and other archaeological specimens which attest that my rev. ancestors first began to act between 1752 and 1829, and we have been at it ever since." He identified William Haycraft Lane (1752–1829) and wife Louisa Rouse (1756–1804) as the "first actors of the tribe."

Louisa Lane arrived in America in 1827 at the age of seven. Daughter of Thomas Frederick Lane, "an actor of considerable provincial fame," and Eliza Trenter Lane, "a very pretty woman and sweet singer of ballads," Louisa was already a veteran of English stages, where she had earned good notices and had learned how delightful it was to her to hold the attention of an audience.

Eliza had given birth to her daughter in Lambeth Parrish, London, in 1820, around the time King George III died. As a symbol of national mourning, theaters remained dark for a month. Players all over England, many of whom lived from hand to mouth even in good times, were hungry and desperate. Most could not even find a friend to borrow from. From this inauspicious beginning Eliza could not have guessed that her first born

daughter would take the talent she inherited from her two performing parents and parlay it into a successful career spanning more than seventy years, or that she would give birth to the maternal half of the first generation of the greatest American family of stage and screen, or that she would care for and cherish her mother until her death in Philadelphia years hence.

Louisa's career began at the age of one year, when her mother carried her on stage in her first role as a "crying baby." Not yet imbued with the sense of responsibility to her fellow players that her practical mother would soon instill, Louisa cooed happily at the audience. "Cry I would not," she wrote, "but at the sight of the audience and the lights gave free vent to my delight and crowed aloud with joy." Just a few years later, however, Louisa was a seasoned trouper. She had played all of the usual children's parts. "I remember (I was about five) playing the rightful heir in a melodrama called 'Meg Murnock' or, the Hag of the Glen.' …After that, in Liverpool, I remember playing the brother of 'Frankenstein,' who is killed by the Monster of Frankenstein's creation," she wrote. Precocious Louisa had traveled so extensively and at such an early age that she was unable to "give any consecutive account" of where she had played.

Louisa's father died before she was five years old, and

Drawing of Miss Louisa Lane at eight years of age portraying five different characters in *Twelve Precisely*.

her only legacy was the long family history of acting. Facing poverty, the new widow found work in local stock companies touring outside London. When she learned of the opportunity to join a British company headed for New York, she wasted no time packing. She and Louisa sailed from London on the packet *Britannia* and arrived in America, "that El Dorado to an imaginative class," four weeks later, in early summer 1827. Mother and daughter spent a few days in New York before being dispatched to America's oldest theater on Walnut Street in Philadelphia.

The building had been erected in 1809 as the New Circus. At the time Eliza and Louisa first saw it, it had an eighty-foot dome that made it the highest structure in the city. In 1811 a stage was added and the name was changed to the Olympic Theater. Thereafter the management changed frequently until, in 1820, the year of Louisa's birth, it became known as the Walnut Street Theater.

The memory of Eliza's American debut at the nation's oldest theater would stay with Louisa until the end of her days. "I remember seeing the 'first appearance' of most of the parties" in the company, Louisa wrote. "Of course my mother's made the finest impression on me. It was as Margaretta in 'No Song, No Supper.' The symphony of her

entrance song is a long one, and the orchestra had to play it twice, her reception was so hearty and her nervousness so great."

Shortly after her American opening, Eliza married Philadelphia actor and stage manager John Kinlock. "From this time my parents' ambition was fixed for me," Louisa explained. "Miss Clara Fisher was then at the zenith of her attraction, and father determined that I should be a second 'Clara.'"

Because of her talent and reputation, Louisa earned the opportunity to support two of the stage's greatest actors. She played the young Duke of York opposite Junius Brutus Booth's Richard III. Louisa was beguiled by the celebrated actor. She had "never heard any one read just like the elder Booth. It was beautiful; he made the figure stand before you! It was infinitely tender." After performing with Booth, Louisa traveled to Baltimore to play the role of Albert II to Edwin Forrest's William Tell. Forrest, still in his early twenties, temperamental as well as talented, was enchanted by the little actress who balanced the apple on her head as he took aim with bow and arrow. At the end of their engagement, Forrest presented her with a silver medal "as a testimonial of his admiration for her talents."

Those talents grew steadily, so that soon Louisa was involved in productions that gave her an opportunity to play a number of different characters in one performance. She played seven roles in *Winning a Husband*, five in *72 Picadilly*, and six in *Actress of All Work*. In 1828 D.C. Johnson drew a caricature of Louisa in the five roles she played in *Twelve Precisely*, and one Philadelphia newspaper highly recommended the entertainment.

> This astonishing little creature…is not more than ten years of age, and evinces a talent for and knowledge of the stage beyond what we find in many experienced performers of merit. The entertainment…is well adapted to the display of the versatility of her powers; and in the *Irish Girl* she may, with truth, be pronounced inimitably comic. Her brogue and manner are excellent. The *Young Soldier* was also admirably assumed; his coxcombical airs were natural, evinced astonishing observation in a child so young, and literally convulsed the house with laughter. Her performance of *Little Pickle* also possessed great merit, and the applause bestowed upon her throughout the evening bespoke the wonder and delight of the audience. Those who have a taste for the wonderful should not miss the present opportunity of gratifying it.

In late 1830 John Kinlock, who was still managing Louisa's career, was "bitten with the idea of management" and set out for Jamaica in charge of a company of actors. They sailed for about ten days before the ship struck a submerged rock. Moonlight sparkled on the calm sea, and the weather was so perfect that Louisa suspected negligence on the part of the crew. She dressed hurriedly and gathered her possessions as the ship took on water.

By morning the passengers and crew were safe on the beach and busy putting up tents. They erected one for the crew, one for the couples, and one for the single gentlemen. (She did not say where she and Eliza slept.) They were lucky: No one was injured in the wreck, and the ship was loaded with wood that could be used for a variety of purposes. They unloaded the supplies from the ship's galley and made themselves reasonably comfortable, expecting an extended stay.

The nearest settlement was estimated to be forty miles away, and the actors were not prepared to travel overland. The company camped on the island for nearly six weeks while the captain traveled to San Domingo to hire a conveyance. Louisa celebrated her eleventh birthday on the beach.

Eventually the group made its way to Kingston, where they enjoyed success until members of the troupe began to fall prey to yellow fever. John Kinlock died, and his pregnant wife lay at death's door. Louisa cared for her mother and her infant half sister, who also succumbed to the fever. Louisa was no doubt petrified of losing her mother and finding herself orphaned in an unfamiliar country. Her mother had, she wrote, "such a siege of illness as for a time to completely prostrate me." Of course, Louisa was not prostrate for long. She took the advice of a kindly doctor and moved with Eliza to the north part of the island, to Falmouth. Louisa found work and Eliza regained her strength. When they became alarmed at rumors of native insurrection, they fled back across the island to Kingston, where they used the money Louisa had earned in Falmouth to book passage to New York.

Philadelphia was most like home to Eliza, so naturally she thought of returning there. From New York, she wrote to the management of the Arch Street Theatre: "Myself and my daughter arrived Sunday from the West Indies, after a voyage of twenty-two days. I presume it is needless to mention Mr. Kinlock's death, as you have doubtless heard of it long before now. Me and Louisa are at liberty to make an engagement with you. Should there be a vacancy I would be most happy to treat with you—that of first singing or singing chamber-maids, indeed a general round of business. As to Louisa, you are aware what she can do. Your answer by return will oblige your obedient and humble servant." William Forrest answered that there were no vacancies at the Arch Street Theatre, but Eliza and her daughter arrived in Philadelphia soon after and began to put down roots.

Eliza found them lodgings at a boardinghouse that was also home to the Fisher family. Louisa made friends with Alexina Fisher, "a very pretty little girl" a year younger than she. "We used to act together in the empty attic room," Louisa recalled, "stab each other with great fury and fall upon the ground, until expostulation from the boarders in the third story caused our reconciliation with tears and embraces." Alexina and Louisa would remain friends for life, and their children would one day marry.

When Louisa was twelve years old, during an engagement in Washington, D.C., she was taken by her host to the President's Levee, where she met Andrew Jackson. "He was very kind and sweet to me," Louisa recounted. He kissed her and complimented her beauty, and from that day forward Louisa was a Jackson Democrat and ardent fan of the man himself.

Louisa Lane Drew, from the frontispiece of her
Autobiographical Sketches of Mrs. John Drew, published
posthumously in 1899.

How often could a talented young actress expect to be shipwrecked? Eliza and Louisa, along with Louisa's half sister Adine Kinlock, were stranded a second time when their ship ran aground on "a sandbar in Egg Harbor," in the West Indies. The night was stormy. They rose quickly and dressed, then stood on deck listening to the creak of the wood, fearing that the planks would let loose. Louisa reported that "Little Adine was quite passive, only saying, 'Mama, if we all go in the water, will God give us breakfast?'"

In the morning they were rescued, but the path to safety was perilous. "We went along the bowsprit with our feet on the rope below, and when we got to the end dropped into the boat the moment it came up on the waves." God didn't let them go into the water, but they "had a long walk in the deep sand to the first house we came to." There they regrouped and eventually decided to pack themselves into a boat carrying building materials and head once again for New York.

The age of thirteen was a trying period for Louisa, for she was "not a child and certainly not a woman." She found herself awkward and less than beautiful. She had put away childish roles as some girls put away their dolls, but at her "very unhappy age" she had to play chambermaids and young boys until she matured into more desirable roles. She had a bit of luck when an actress fell ill and she was tapped to play a chambermaid with a well-known comedian of the day. She "sang a little song called 'Nice Young Maiden' for forty-eight successive nights, and was very happy." Her song was always encored. Then, "Mother, being ambitious for me, accepted an engagement in Boston...where we jointly received a salary of $16 per week." They "passed a very happy two seasons in the enjoyment of that large salary."

Louisa admired her mother's practical approach. She "was a splendid manager" and "a marvelously industrious woman." In Boston, Eliza found shelter for them at a comfortable boardinghouse. Louisa found the large second-story room cozy, with its trundle bed and a closet large enough to hold a barrel of ale and their entire wardrobe.

At this time actors had a very different lot from the traditions of support, fringe benefits, and deference that grew up after players began to interest the public as individuals. At the time Eliza and Louisa were touring players, actors were thought to be somewhat unsavory and inclined to behave in less civilized ways than more stationary citizens. But actors worked hard: They provided their own room and board, purchased their own meals, paid their own travel costs, and supplied their own costumes. Rather than attending parties after hours, most players were at home engaged in learning lines, mending their street clothes (which doubled as costumes), and stretching their food and money as far as they would go. To accomplish all this for herself and her two children, Eliza must have been a superior manager indeed.

Eliza instilled in her daughter a life-long sense of responsibility for herself, her family, and her profession. "The show must go on" was not just a quaint theater saying to Louisa. She would work tirelessly her entire life to support and sustain herself, her children, their children, her mother, her half sisters, and various orphans and friends.

Eliza was also steadfastly religious and passed this trait on to her daughter. They had the courage of their convictions, and occasionally they would lose work because they would never have dreamed of performing on the Sabbath. Regardless of the prevailing view of stage people as common and lacking in morals, Eliza was strict about Louisa's upbringing and made sure she was chaperoned at all times. "Nothing can compensate a well brought up girl for loss of home and all that word means," Louisa wrote, but she never voiced any complaints about the life that was chosen for her.

By the age of fifteen Louisa had moved up to playing what she described as "several young mothers of the rightful heirs." She recalled "what a delight it was then to drag a little child after me during three long acts, to have him wrenched from my arms, torn away in despite of my unearthly shrieks to summon my faithful page...who undertook to find him and punish the 'wretches who had stolen him,' and always succeeded after many hair-breadth escapes in the 'imminent deadly breach!'" As always, Louisa's enthusiasm for her work is evident in her writing about it.

At the age of sixteen, Louisa married Henry Blaine Hunt, whom she described as "a very good singer, a nice actor, and a very handsome man of forty." Hunt, who had once been in the entourage of George IV, was an Irish comedian who had lost his appeal in England and was touring America, where audiences didn't hold his political views against him. Eliza and Louisa knew him by reputation, though they had not moved in his circles in London. He must have appealed to Louisa as a secure, mature man would to a girl who had been working hard to support her family since before she could remember.

For a while, the Hunts and the Kinlocks toured together, but gradually Hunt dropped out of the group and went his own way. Louisa was now recognized as a leading lady and, for reasons she did not disclose, marriage to Hunt held no more appeal for her. She secured an engagement at the Walnut Street Theatre in Philadelphia, site of her mother's American debut, "at the highest salary known there, $20 per week." She toured again the following year, the same year she divorced Hunt.

In 1849, Louisa joined the Albany Museum company and met and married George Mossop, an Irish comedian but a poor imitation of Hunt, lacking his "dashing manners and great animal spirits." Mossop left Louisa a widow after less than a year of marriage. Soon after, Louisa set her cap for the third—and last—Irish comedian she would marry.

The Drews

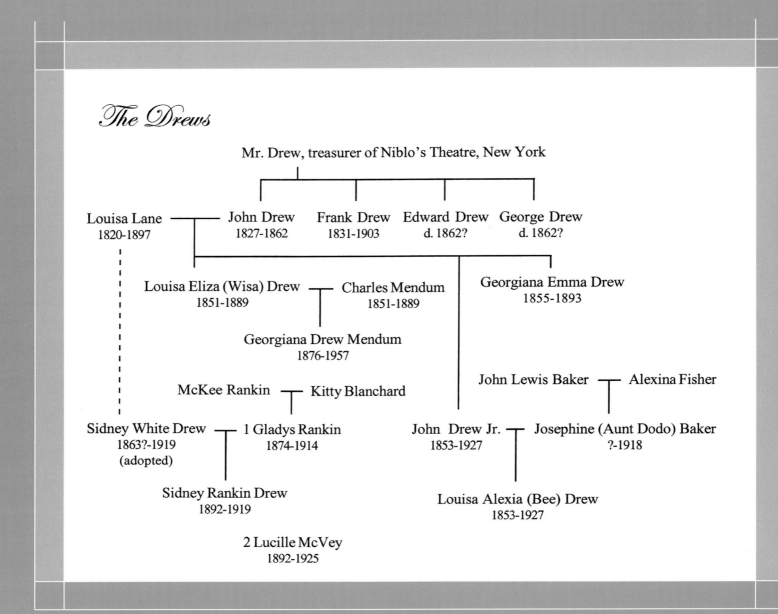

Mr. Drew, treasurer of Niblo's Theatre, New York

Louisa Lane
1820-1897

John Drew
1827-1862

Frank Drew
1831-1903

Edward Drew
d. 1862?

George Drew
d. 1862?

Louisa Eliza (Wisa) Drew
1851-1889

Charles Mendum
1851-1889

Georgiana Emma Drew
1855-1893

Georgiana Drew Mendum
1876-1957

John Lewis Baker — Alexina Fisher

McKee Rankin — Kitty Blanchard

Sidney White Drew
1863?-1919
(adopted)

1 Gladys Rankin
1874-1914

John Drew Jr.
1853-1927

Josephine (Aunt Dodo) Baker
?-1918

Sidney Rankin Drew
1892-1919

Louisa Alexia (Bee) Drew
1853-1927

2 Lucille McVey
1892-1925

The Drews

The theatre is not a building or an aggregate of buildings in which theatrical performances are given, but a social institution, like Literature, or any other form of Art.

—THEATER CRITIC WILLIAM WINTER

IN 1837, THE PATRIARCH of the Drew family boarded a ship in Dublin with his wife and six children. They traveled to New York, where Mr. Drew eventually found work as the treasurer of a theater on Broadway. His children were allowed the run of the theater, a privilege that had a tendency to demystify some aspects of the profession while making other aspects very appealing. But the stage had no attraction for one of Drew's sons, John, who announced at the age of thirteen that he was going to sea. His father evidently found that suitable work for the restless young man, and he signed his son on as apprentice on a whaler.

After several years as a sailor, John Drew returned to New York determined to make his second career on the stage. But the stage was not kindly disposed toward him at that time. He found work at a ragged theater where he gained more experience than wages but was retired when the company went bankrupt. The parts he found after that were discouraging and, rather than starve, he next tried his hand as a merchant. Relatives helped him set up a small dry goods shop in Dublin, and he did well until he become embroiled in local politics. He shortly sailed again for America.

This time he would let nothing stand in his way: He was determined to make a reputation for himself on the stage. Parts were easier to find this time, and his portrayals were hailed as original. He played traditional Irish characters, but "his voice, manner, and abandon invest such characters with life," read one New York review. He played a season in Rochester and toured the next year before joining the Albany Museum company, where Eliza, Louisa, and her half sister Georgiana were already engaged.

IN 1850, JOHN DREW was twenty-two years old. He was a bit shorter than average height, slender of build, with dark hair and sparkling black eyes. His musical voice carried a promise of laughter. He was a spellbinding storyteller, friendly and open in social situations, and overly generous and soft-hearted. He liked everyone, and the feeling was returned.

Georgiana Kinlock was eighteen years old. Louisa's little half sister had grown beautiful. She lacked Louisa's business acumen, and she regarded herself much less seriously than her sister took herself. She was flirtatious, and she had taken a shine to John Drew. Drew was not difficult to approach, and it was soon clear that he returned Georgiana's feelings. John asked Eliza if he could begin to court her youngest daughter, and Eliza was inclined to allow it, until she consulted Louisa. Her eldest daughter,

Portrait of Mrs. John Drew, whose career lasted more than
seventy years.

who had already decided that she and John Drew would
make a formidable theatrical couple, gave a number of
reasons why the courtship was not acceptable.

At thirty years old, Louisa had established her reputation as an actress and was commanding leading roles and
earning top dollar. She was not conventionally beautiful,
but she made people forget that. Her voice was rich and
musical, and she had a gift for projecting it, using it to
make audiences fall in love with her characters. She could
play comedy or tragedy, and she could also sing and
dance. She had an hourglass figure and huge blue eyes
that were cool and intelligent. She wore her long, dark
hair pulled back and draped softly around her ears. She
seemed to take up more space than her five-foot-tall frame

should require, and she intimidated more than a few of
her many acquaintances. She usually got what she wanted,
and what she wanted was John Drew.

So, in July 1850, Louisa married the gentle, restless
Irishman she fancied, although the merger wasn't made
public for several months because Louisa had to fulfill her
schedule of engagements before she could begin to tour
with her husband. Publications of the day suggested that
Drew had made the best engagement he'd ever made by
marrying the talented trouper. Georgiana Kinlock's reaction
was not recorded.

Mr. and Mrs. John Drew had no shortage of offers. They
played together their first season in Chicago and the next
in Buffalo. The reputation Louisa had established for her-

John Drew Sr.
as Handy Andy,
one of his best
known roles.

An engraving of
John Drew Sr.
in costume.

self elevated her new husband. John, because of his affable personality, was popular everywhere they went, and Louisa was welcomed with warmth and respect. Her inner warmth was not readily apparent to casual acquaintances, but those who knew her well recognized that "beneath her reserve and surface sternness there was an emotional, tender heart as responsive as a child's to any claim upon its sympathies," according to one family friend.

One of Drew's most famous roles was that of Handy Andy, in which he was called "incomparably comic." The *Dublin Express* reported that "he was dressed, looked and acted the part with consumate taste, rich comic humor, and perfect success, drawing down peals of cheering laughter throughout the entire piece." The *Irish Times* also commended his ability, reporting that "the audience seemed to forget he was acting, and looked upon the most faithful and original picture of an Irishman ever."

The Drews found work in Philadelphia at the Chestnut Street Theatre, where they attracted audiences and garnered praise. Louisa gave birth to a daughter, whom she named after herself and called "Wisa." Louisa began to dream of settling down and raising her family in one place. About the same time, William Wheatley tried to interest John Drew in sharing the lease on the Arch Street Theatre, and Louisa strongly urged him toward that

course. She had great affection for the city of Philadelphia, and she wanted to stay.

In August 1853 the Arch Street Theatre opened under Drew's and Wheatley's management, and their first production was a success. Mrs. Drew had been unable to perform because she was otherwise engaged. She gave birth to John ("Jack") Drew Jr. in November and returned a month later to perform under her husband's management in a variety of roles, all of which brought her good notices. Their *Comedy of Errors* turned out to be a family gathering, with John and Louisa, Frank Drew—who looked enough like his brother that Louisa had at least once confused them—and Eliza and Georgiana Kinlock in the cast.

Ever-restless John Drew tired of managing a theater. In 1855 he arranged for a starring tour of England and Ireland and invited his mother-in-law to accompany him. Mrs. Kinlock was so excited with the prospect of seeing her native land again that Louisa softened a little toward her husband's scheme. But she didn't let Eliza or John know that she was pregnant again, and as a result father and grandmother would not see the younger Drew daughter, Georgiana Emma, until she was more than a year old.

Louisa was businesslike and mature; John was not practical, and he indulged the children more than his wife

Miniature portrait of Louisa Lane Drew, at one time owned by her son Jack and reproduced in her autobiography.

approved. Jack Drew reported that one of his first memories was of "an Irish donkey that was allowed to roam for a short time in our back yard" before being sold to someone who perhaps had a real use for a beast of burden. John Senior had come home from his first world tour with the animal, intending to make it a pet for the children. One can imagine practical Louisa shaking her head at such an acquisition. She did not reveal exactly how she felt about the casual easiness with which her husband moved through his days, but throughout her life she would show a preference for unconventional men with a reputation for being naughty, and she did possess a keen sense of irony. Perhaps she was secretly amused.

In 1857, John Drew tried management again, but with poor results. He gave up the lease on the Arch Street Theatre, and the Drews played the 1858 season at the Walnut Street Theatre. John began to dream of a second world tour, including "California by way of the Isthmus and from there…to Australia and then to London and Ireland."

John did not have the high aspirations for himself that Louisa had for him. She encouraged him to stretch and develop his talents, but he was content to enjoy life and

find peace and good companionship where he could. As they would remain to the end, Louisa wanted security, and John wanted travel and change. They would never agree on the priority of their pursuits, but Louisa would try to accommodate John's wanderlust when it did not interfere with her plans for security and family.

No one knows for sure why Mrs. Drew sent her sister Georgiana Kinlock, who had at one time been in love with John Drew, on tour with her husband, but in 1859 they embarked on another world tour, taking eight-year-old Wisa along. The travelers would not return for three years, and when they did they would bring with them a small shock for Louisa.

WHILE HER HUSBAND traveled, Louisa played a season at the Arch Street Theatre under the management of Wheatley and Clarke. Then, in 1860, the stockholders of the theater asked Louisa to manage it for the coming season. The job would not be easy—the Arch was mired in debt. Louisa wrote to her husband in Ireland to make sure he had no objections to her becoming one of the few female theater managers in the country. He did not.

Portrait of John Drew Sr. at the height of his career. He died at the age of thirty-six from a combination of illness and a fall down the stairs.

The Arch Street Theatre had been built in 1827 and, as Mrs. Drew saw it, was due for some renovations. It was the second oldest playhouse in America, a stately Greek temple designed by architect Walter Strickland. "The building had pillars outside like the old Greek Parthenon and inside it was all red velvet and gold," Ethel Barrymore recalled. The first season of Louisa's management, minor renovations were undertaken. Louisa had a difficult time paying her employees that year, and she had to borrow to make the payroll.

Under Mrs. Drew's management, the Arch Street Theatre thrived and soon boasted a fine stock company. Famous players sought engagements there, and they enjoyed working at the location because it was clean, well-run, and orderly. The facility had ten dressing rooms and would seat 1,911 people. By Louisa's third season, stock values had risen and a complete remodeling was planned "from the stage to the front door."

According to Jack Drew, "a day in the Arch Street Theatre started with a rehearsal which began at ten o'clock in the morning and lasted about four hours." At two o'clock Louisa returned home, and at three o'clock she had dinner and then retired. Usually players had their afternoons free for study and rest. She would be back at the theater when the doors opened. Performances began at eight o'clock each evening—except Sundays—and on Saturday they gave a matinee. Every evening after the performance, Louisa had a light supper in her room and followed that with a little rye whiskey to induce sleep.

The Drew children were not allowed back stage at the theater, except when they "entered the family box from the stage so as to avoid the crowds in the lobby." Friday was usually their theater night, and their grandmother usually accompanied them to the manager's box, where they saw every great actor and actress of the day. "We sat in a box marked 'D' and only Mumum had the key," Ethel wrote.

RIGHT AFTER CHRISTMAS 1861, John Drew returned to Philadelphia with Georgiana and Wisa. At their house on Buttonwood Street, Louisa and Eliza welcomed the travelers. Wisa was almost a young lady. John was as handsome as ever. The shock came when Georgiana revealed a small baby. John tried to explain: Georgiana had married an actor they met in Melbourne, but this Robert L. Stephens had not met them in England as they had planned. The infant was a product of the brief union.

Louisa accepted the bundle that was offered her, named the baby Adine (after frail half sister Adine, who had died by this time) Kinlock Stephens Drew, and announced she would raise the child as her adopted daughter. (Georgiana would die in 1864 when little Adine was two years old.)

After he returned, John Drew played one hundred performances at the Arch Street Theatre under his wife's management. Little did they realize that this would be his last engagement. When his run of performances ended, he took a short business trip to New York and returned feeling ill. Three days later, on Georgiana's sixth birthday, he died. The *Philadelpia Press* reported that

> taking a child in his arms in his own house, on Tuesday, his foot caught in the carpet, throwing Mr. Drew in such a manner that his head struck a wall, and he became utterly senseless. Convulsions ensued, and a physician was summoned, but his aid was unavailing. Mr. Drew suffered until yesterday afternoon, when he expired at four o'clock. By his decease the Stage has been deprived of one of its most amusing and accomplished Actors, and all Philadelphians—for his greatest achievements were identified with our city—can share the afflictions of his family.

Wisa Drew showed no interest in becoming an actress, but by 1874, spirited Georgiana and her handsome brother Jack were playing light comedy at their mother's Arch Street Theatre. Augustin Daly, famous playwright and theatrical manager, saw them on a visit to the Arch and was so impressed that he wrote to Louisa with offers for them to join his New York company. Jack accepted. Georgie decided to stay near her mother for the coming season because theater traditions were changing in ways that disheartened Louisa.

Jack Drew opened in New York in January 1875 under the management of Augustin Daly in *The Big Bonanza.* The program informed the audience that, "aside from his own merits," he should be made welcome on the New York stage "on account of the fame of his mother, the celebrated Philadelphia actress and manageress, and the memory of his father, who was one of the best Irish comedians of his day."

Georgie stayed in Philadelphia, where she played leading lady to a number of talented male stars engaged as special attractions by Mrs. Drew. She could have received

The Arch Street Theatre in Philadelphia, where Mrs. John Drew made her name as one of the country's first female theater managers. She ran the concern for more than thirty years, until the star system made stock companies obsolete.

no better training than to spend a season under her mother's management and tutelage. Georgiana was striking with her huge blue eyes and curly golden hair, and she had a natural manner of acting. She was a sparkling wit and was fast becoming the darling of Philadelphia audiences, but none of the men she brought to tea was good enough for her, and her mother made sure that she understood that.

DURING HIS FIRST SEASON at Daly's Fifth Avenue Theatre, Jack Drew met a handsome wit named Maurice Barrymore. He spoke in the clipped tones of an educated Englishman, and he was an expert on male pursuits—an amateur boxing champion, an aficionado of the new bicycle craze, an experienced swimmer and rower. Jack,

Jack Drew inherited his father's skill at charming audiences. He eventually became known as "the first gentleman of the American theater."

Georgiana Emma Drew, younger daughter of one of the country's favorite theater families, began her career as a teenager on her mother's Arch Street stage in Philadelpia.

an avid sportsman himself, and "Barry," as Barrymore was called, became fast friends.

Barry found New York to his liking. He rose early to run or swim, he trained with Billy Muldoon, sparred with whatever partner he could find at the gym, and had philosophical discussions with his idol, boxer John L. Sullivan. Barry spent his evenings at drinking establishments where players and writers gathered. When he wanted female companionship, he found a number of ravishing volunteers.

The next time Daly asked Georgie to come to New York, she accepted. Like her mother, she had a way of captivating audiences. After her training at the Arch, she was ready for the New York stage. Her goal was to gain recognition there as she had in her hometown. Her first day at the Fifth Avenue Theatre, Augustin Daly introduced her to the company. He saw, as did everyone in the green room, how Georgie's glittering blue eyes fastened on Barry's gray ones as they greeted one another for the first time.

Mischievous Georgie Drew was the favorite of her formidable mother, and of her siblings she seems to have been the one most like her mother.

GEORGIE'S FIRST SEASON in New York was ending, and she had been an undisputed success at Daly's Fifth Avenue Theatre. She and her brother Jack had already signed contracts for the next three seasons, but Barry was unsure of his future even though Daly had offered him leading roles at good pay. After an amazingly long run of *Pique*, holding Georgie in his arms on stage every night but Sunday and twice on Saturday, he knew that he was captivated with Miss Drew. He found himself spending all his spare time with her and dragging Jack along as chaperon. When Jack invited Barry to join the Drew family in Philadelphia for the month between theatrical seasons, he readily accepted.

In short order, most of the Drew family were hopelessly enamored of the delightful Englishman. He was handsome, intelligent, and quick with his tongue, something the Drews were known for too. Barry impressed Grandmother Kinlock—who became flirtatious and coy with the handsome guest—little Adine, Sidney Drew, and the maid, but imperious Mrs. John Drew was a little more difficult to win over.

One lovely day as Maurice and Georgie strolled in the old Revolutionary War cemetery across from the Drew family home, Barry formally proposed, and Georgie formally accepted. Later, when they asked for Mrs. Drew's consent, she looked at the hopeful suitor. "And what are your professional plans for the future, Mr. Barrymore?" she asked. Startled by the question, Barry quickly committed himself to the three-season contract that Daly had offered him. He was going to have a good salary and leading parts in the Fifth Avenue Theatre, he explained. Perhaps Mrs. Drew nodded, and perhaps she merely looked away.

When Georgie set her big blue eyes on Maurice Barrymore for the first time in Daly's green room, she decided to make Barry a priority along with her career.

THE NEXT BREAK AT THE Fifth Avenue Theatre, which happened to be over the holiday season, Barry and Georgie took the opportunity to find a minister. Mrs. Drew had not warmed to Barry, but she was holding her tongue. "Miss Georgiana Emma Drew, the youngest daughter of the late John Drew, was united in the bonds of holy matrimony on the 31st day of December 1876, to Maurice Herbert Blyth (Barrymore) of London, Esq., at the residence of the bride's mother in Philadelphia, the Rev. Dr. Rudder, rector of St. Stephen's Church, in that city, officiating on this happy occasion," wrote a *New York Clipper* reporter, who added, "We wish them all possible prosperity on their new roles in *Married Life.*"

Louisa had consented to the marriage because she loved Georgie fiercely and wanted her to be happy. After all, she had chosen a man who was very similar to those Louisa had chosen for herself. She may have understood her spirited daughter's choice, but she still worried about her future. Mrs. Drew never did warm to her son-in-law; even though Barry and Georgie made a striking couple, Mrs. Drew recognized in Barry that indolent charm that had prevented John Drew from becoming the equal of a Booth or a Jefferson.

And what do we really know about this Maurice Barrymore? Mrs. Drew wondered.

Mrs. John Drew as Mrs. Malaprop in Sheridan's *The Rivals.* After she left the Arch Street Theatre, she toured in the role for many years, playing opposite Joseph Jefferson.

Dapper John Drew attracted audiences who were as keen to see his wardrobe as they were his acting ability.

HOLLIS ST. THEATRE PROGRAM   WEEK OF MARCH 8, 1903

HOLLIS ST. THEATRE
MONDAY, MARCH 23.
2 WEEKS ENGAGEMENT Matinees Wednesday and Saturday.
CHARLES FROHMAN PRESENTS

JOHN DREW
IN
"The Mummy and The Humming Bird."

An advertisement for *The Mummy and the Hummingbird,* in which John Drew starred and his nephew Lionel Barrymore made his stage debut. Lionel upstaged his famous uncle with his authentic portrayal of an organ grinder.

John Drew at his writing desk. He once received a letter from Samuel Clemens claiming that his children were impressed with him not because of his writing talent but because of his acquaintance with Drew.

A John Drew cigar band. Most people thought he owned an interest in the company that produced John Drew cigars, but his name was used without his permission, and he did not benefit at all from their sale.

Louisa Lane Drew's adopted son Sidney, who was known to the Barrymore children as "Uncle Googan." Mr. and Mrs. Sidney (Gladys Rankin) Drew were popular for their many short marital comedies.

Soon after the death of his first wife, Sidney Drew met Lucille McVey, a Vitagraph writer half his age. They married immediately and worked together until Sidney's death about five years later. This advertisement is for *Once a Mason* (1919), a comedy they wrote and produced for Paramount.

SIDNEY DREW   Vitagraph Player

Sidney Drew postcard from the time he worked for Vitagraph. Sidney's heart was broken when his only child, S. Rankin Drew, a talented director who was building a successful career of his own before he enlisted, was killed in action in World War I. Sidney Sr. did not survive long after his son's death.

The Blyths

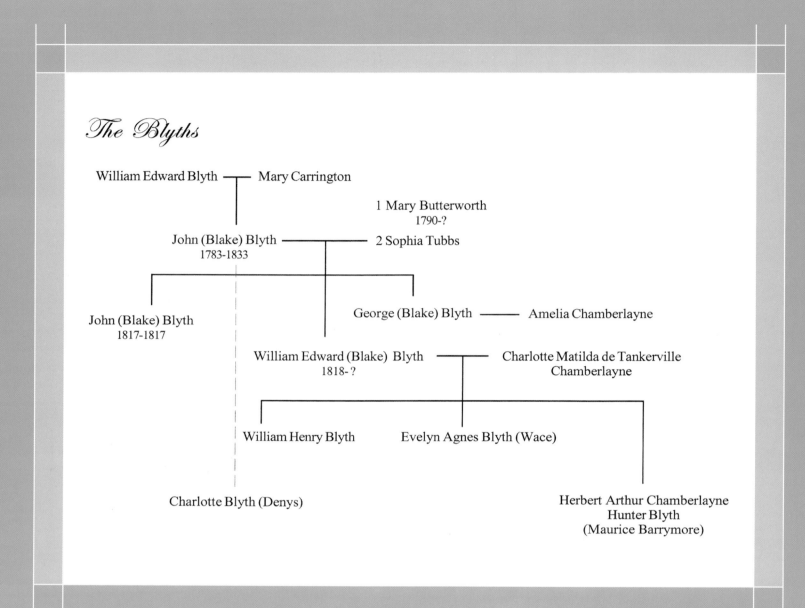

William Edward Blyth ——— Mary Carrington

John (Blake) Blyth ———
1783-1833

1 Mary Butterworth
1790-?

2 Sophia Tubbs

John (Blake) Blyth
1817-1817

George (Blake) Blyth ——— Amelia Chamberlayne

William Edward (Blake) Blyth ——— Charlotte Matilda de Tankerville
1818-?   Chamberlayne

William Henry Blyth   Evelyn Agnes Blyth (Wace)

Charlotte Blyth (Denys)

Herbert Arthur Chamberlayne
Hunter Blyth
(Maurice Barrymore)

The Blyths

How in good faith could I be aunt to an actor on the stage?

—AMELIA BLYTH

THE NAME "MAURICE BARRYMORE" was a relatively recent invention. Before Barry changed his name, he had been Herbert Blyth. And he was not the first of the Blyth line to change his name to avoid embarrassment.

IN 1783 WILLIAM EDWARD BLYTH and his wife, the former Mary Carrington, had their first child. By 1800, twelve more had been born to the couple. The family lived in Sneating Hall, Essex, a rented estate, because Blyth's older brother had inherited Beaumont Hall, the family place. Blyth took great pleasure in the fact that Sneating Hall sat on a hill above the original family home. Even though he had to use his wife's dowry to secure the property, he was able to look down on his brother's estate as often as he liked.

Blyth believed that education was the way to advancement, and he wanted his children raised as ladies and gentlemen. He hired a tutor, who singled out second son John as the potential scholar. John, an adventurer at heart, had other plans.

He fancied himself in love with the daughter of one of his father's cottagers. Immediately before he was to start his education at Christ Church, he learned that his lady love was with child. To his credit, John announced to his father that he planned to marry the girl who was carrying his child.

As expected, Blyth the elder was not about to agree to such a scheme. He paid the cottager to take his family and leave in the dead of night. When John learned what had happened, he stole his father's best horse and took off in the direction of London.

As any eighteen year old reared in the country, John was staggered by the immense city, which he had only visited briefly in the past in the company of his father. Now he was free to explore and of the very age to appreciate his freedom the most.

John found compatriots in the taverns of London, and through one he heard of a generous, amorous widow who was searching for a boarder. In the bargain, John gained a wardrobe courtesy of the widow's late husband. John's new landlady was past her prime, but, in return for John's favors, she waived the rent.

While living with the widow, John established himself as a tutor to children of nearby merchants, though he still longed for adventure. At night he frequented drinking establishments and brothels, and the widow grew tired of his wanderings. Eventually John left rather than entertain the widow's offers of marriage. He made straight for the docks of the East India Company and

Herbert Blyth about the time he took the name Maurice Herbert Barrymore. He saw the surname on a playbill at the Haymarket in London shortly before he sailed to America.

was soon aboard the *Tigris*, headed for Calcutta as assistant to the purser.

During the voyage, John befriended young men in the Company's pay and found himself stirred by their enthusiasm for the new life they were to start in India. John decided that living in a wild, unfamiliar country full of opportunity would suit him better than life aboard the *Tigris*. He developed a simple plan. When the ship docked, John went ashore with his comrades, wearing the entire wardrobe he had inherited from the widow's former spouse. He never returned to the ship.

The English in Calcutta had attempted to establish a British society despite the climate, which was unfriendly to those who insisted on wearing wigs, brocades, and corsets. Disease killed 80 percent of the Europeans who settled in the colony. Some turned to drink and native women, tired of the heat and the strain of living as Englishmen on foreign shores. The Bengal artillery kept the interior secure, and an army of surveyors and civil servants measured and mapped the vast land.

Shortly after John went ashore, he changed his surname to Blake. John Blake became a non-commissioned officer in the Honourable Company's European Army on the Bengal Establishment, and he was sent to Fort Williams as a writer. After a few years he was transferred to the Lower Orphan School, where they needed someone to teach Latin and Greek.

At the school, John Blake met twenty-two-year-old Mary Butterworth, daughter of a Bengal army officer. She was headstrong and willful, as John was, and she had for years been refusing offers of marriage. They were married in the summer of 1812, in the chapel at Fort William Garrison. Their first child died shortly after she was born, and Mary died giving birth to a second daughter, who survived only a short time after her mother's death.

Eventually the British crown took over the ruling of India, and John's station seemed less respected than it had in the heyday of the Honourable East India Company. He tried to go back to his old social habits of frequenting taverns and enjoying the nightlife of the city. But he began to lose interest in society altogether.

In 1816 John Blake married Sophia Tubbs, a beautiful woman of questionable background. She was dark with soft features and a shy manner that came in part from the awe in which she held her husband.

John and Sophia had their first son in 1817. John Junior was a sickly child who did not survive long. In 1818 a second son, William Edward, was born, and he was healthy and bright.

As his father had, John insisted that his children be educated, and he used a method of repetition and brow-beating that did little to endear him to his children. Second son William Edward showed an aptitude for learning that did not escape his father's notice.

About this time John began to hear gossip about his wife, who was said to be the offspring of a Bengal army officer and a native Indian woman, a combination English society in Calcutta found distasteful. To put distance between his family and the sources of the rumors, John took a position at the Fort at Allabad and moved his family to the point where the Jumna River joins the Ganges.

The rigorous education of William Edward and his seven siblings continued. Their father was determined that they should be prepared for life by becoming ladies and gentlemen. To facilitate that end, he dropped the name Blake, and in 1828 the family became Blyths again in hopes of reestablishing the connection to their birthright.

John Blyth died of typhoid fever in 1833. Before he expired, he told William Edward about Essex and of his father, and how it was that he ran away. He urged his son to write to Sneating Hall and tell his relatives what had become of the son who rode off toward London years before.

William Edward became head of the household. Through the concern of a sympathetic surveyor who noticed a spark of something in William, he was offered a revenue surveying position. The young man was quietly patient and very intelligent. His ability was rewarded with promotion as other positions became available.

At the age of twenty, a surveying assignment took him to Ghazipur, a city that was fragrant with the scent of roses, where rose water and attar of roses was manufactured. He met and married Charlotte Matilda de Tankerville Chamberlayne, daughter of the local apothecary, Henry Chamberlayne, an Irishman who loved the art of conversation. Matilda was sixteen and attractive, with flashing green eyes and fine bones. She liked to twine white roses in her dark hair.

Matilda traveled with William on assignments, and they made their home wherever William was sent. They had three children. The first died at the age of one year and one month, but William Henry and Evelyn Agnes survived. The senior William moved the family to Amritsar in 1846.

In 1849, Matilda announced that she was expecting another child. She had already decided that she was having a son, and she asked family friends James and Sarah Hunter to be his godparents. The pregnancy was difficult, and Matilda did not survive it.

Herbert Arthur Chamberlayne Hunter Blyth, on September 21, 1849, "was born in the dungeons of Fort Agra during the Mutiny," wrote Ethel Barrymore. Herbert would spend his early years running free with his dog Rahj, hunting with his uncle George, exploring with the native Indian boys. He was raised by his Aunt Amelia, sister to Matilda and wife of William's brother George.

Eventually William did write the letter to Sneating Hall. The old squire had died years before, and his offspring had regained the family estate. The letter was answered by Charlotte Blyth Denys, the youngest of the squire's children. Any of William Edward's children whom he wished to send to England for schooling would be most welcome at Beaumont Hall, Charlotte wrote.

Because Amelia Blyth wanted to get Herbert off the streets of Amritsar, where he was learning something other than gentlemanly conduct, arrangements were made for him to take the exams for Harrow. He did very well, and left for England in the fall of 1860 at the age of eleven. He was accompanied by his aunt and uncle as far as Calcutta, where he boarded the *Nile* with eight other boys traveling with a tutor to school in England.

Herbert attended Blackheath Preparatory School at Harrow. He was intelligent and was a good scholar when he applied himself, but the colonial boy was often busy defending himself from the taunts and bullying of his peers. And his pugilistic talents were nothing to sneer at—he was an expert in fisticuffs from running with the ragged pack of Indian boys, an advantage none of his tormentors had.

The summer of 1861 Herbert went to Beaumont Hall, where his brother William was staying with Aunt Charlotte between school sessions. Will was nearly sixteen by then, and a virtual stranger to Herbert, though he bore a strong resemblance to their father.

Their aunt, Charlotte Denys, was tall and thin. In the face she looked a little like Herbert's grandfather, who had fled from Essex so long before. Aunt and nephew took a liking to each other and spent many hours that summer walking in the countryside.

To the disgust of his stern father, Herbert had been asked not to return to school after the summer break. His father sent him a letter expressing his disappointment that his son had squandered his chances. "I lament the waste of the opportunities set before you," he wrote. "I have sent you to Harrow, a school for the sons of gentlemen, so you will be able to meet them on equal ground in the Great World, but instead you brawl like a guttersnipe and ignore your studies." He then made other arrangements for his wayward son.

In the fall, Herbert and his brother lodged together at the house of Mrs. Valentine, widow of a school proprietor who employed a tutor and offered room and board to a few promising scholars at a time. Rather than being put in the special department that trained for civil service, Herbert was enrolled in classic studies, at which he proved a capable student.

When he finished classes at Harrow, Herbert went on to Lincoln College, Oxford. He discovered a love of sports and became amateur boxing champion. "He began to read for the bar," according to Ethel Barrymore, but he couldn't shake off his attraction for the stage. His family, says Ethel, "recoiled in horror as only Victorian Anglo-Indians could."

As Lionel Barrymore recalls the story his father told him, the start of his father's career, like his own, came about through the sheerest luck. "One evening I was strolling along the pier at Brighton when my notice was attracted by the plight of an elderly gentleman who was escorting an exceedingly pretty jeune fille," the story began.

> As if the aged buck were not already in enough difficulty, as you will understand someday, he was beset by dock loafers who were making insulting remarks to and about the young lady.
>
> Noble fellow that I am, I intervened and bade the scamps be about their business. Upon discovering they were unbiddable, I naturally knocked their heads together, a matter which required little effort on my part in those days, and having done my good turn for the evening was about to depart. But my elderly friend introduced himself as Charles Vandenhoff, the comedian, and invited me to have a repast with him. Of course I accepted, always being in the mood for a dinner, and the upshot of that pleasant engagement was that I confessed to Mr. Vanderhoff that I had lightly considered becoming an actor. He encouraged me, commended my stage presence, particularly when it

came to knocking heads together, and so I made the decision. You see, my boys, it was not entirely without a touch of gallantry that your father entered upon his noble profession.

HERBERT HADN'T YET SETTLED on a plan for his future. After intense training, he won the amateur middle weight championship of England. While he was studying for the bar, circumstances conspired to get him on the stage, and he found that he liked it, fight as he might against a career that would displease his family. He began to travel about the provinces with his friend, comedian Charles Vandenhoff, serving his apprenticeship playing valets, detectives, and other minor characters.

As expected, the Blyth family did not approve of Herbert's activities, and they did not hesitate to make it clear. Herbert's Aunt Amelia, whom the young man loved dearly, surprised him by writing with candor to express her disapproval. About Herbert's father, she wrote, "He must never know that his youngest child by my lamented sister has ventured upon the stage, for it would be the end of that good man, and the end of many things, I fear." Of all the expressions of disapproval that Herbert received, this one must have stung the most.

To prevent shame from falling on his family, Herbert decided to change his name. At first he simply added an "e" to the end of his surname, then he performed several times as "G.H. Blyth" before he hit upon the name of Barrymore, taken from an old playbill. "Maurice" sounded gentlemanly and provided a bit of dash. (He wanted the name to be pronounced in the manner of the French, but English pronunciation turned it into "Morris.") Herbert made a nice middle name. His friends immediately shortened the new name to "Barry."

Ethel gave the romantic version of the situation. "So he gaily promised to find another name and do his damnest in America," she wrote. "So off he went with his beauty, his charm, and his wit to conquer the new world and make his fortune." While Ethel's telling is in keeping with Barry's spirit, his adventures must have been dampened by the fact that his career choice had alienated him from his entire family, and most of them would never approve of him or forgive him.

THE YEAR WAS 1875 when Maurice Barrymore arrived in Boston, having left Herbert Blyth on the shore of England. Barry had an inheritance from his aunt Charlotte Denys and a willing compatriot in Charley Vandenhoff, so he took his time finding work. He explored the city with elderly actor William Warren during the day, and the taverns and saloons with Vandenhoff in the evenings.

In January he acted the part of the lead in *Under the Gaslight* at a benefit for actor C. Leslie Allen. He was soon invited to appear as Captain Molyneux in Dion Boucicault's *The Shaughraun,* which the author (and star) would direct.

Boucicault gave Barry a hard time at first, but that was not unusual for the actor. Despite his unappreciated direction, he and Barry soon became friends. And Barry was, if not a great actor, at least greatly admired for his physical attributes, even by the critic for the *Evening Transcript.* Barry's "broad shoulders, manly stride, clean-cut features, handsome teeth, gentlemanly bearing and refined self-possession" caused the *Transcript* writer to predict that he would become the object of many young ladies' desire. That was already true, and it remained true until the end of Barry's life. It was "a role well fitted to his splendid physique and personal magnetism. He was talented as well as handsome, and it was not long before he made his presence felt on the boards of the Broadway rialto," wrote biographer Alma Power-Waters.

AUGUSTIN DALY OFFERED Barry $75 a week to start, and the actor arrived in New York shortly after accepting.

He reported to Daly's Fifth Avenue Theatre in the heart of a city that already compared favorably to London as far as the Englishman was concerned. Daly assigned Barry to his touring company, and the manager went along on the trip by rail to San Francisco. Barry did not last very long on tour, and Daly soon sent him back to the Fifth Avenue to rehearse the role of Bob Ruggles in *The Big Bonanza.* Daly hoped the handsome Barrymore could compete with popular H.J. Montague, the stage idol who was packing in ladies at Wallack's matinees. He could, and did.

By December Barry and Fanny Davenport were pulling Daly's theater back into the black with their performances in *Pique,* in which Barry played a charming villain with gusto. They soon added matinees, at which ladies of leisure could swoon over Barry afternoons. For the one-hundreth performance of *Pique,* Daly organized the entire week around his "Gala Centennial Celebration." The theater was decorated, special matinees were offered, and souvenir programs on pink satin were distributed. Copies of a photograph of the handsome villain embracing the leading lady were given away, and Daly's musical director composed a special "Pique Waltz." Barry was a star.

Soon Miss Georgiana Drew would report to the Fifth Avenue Theatre, and Mr. Maurice Herbert Barrymore's heart would never again be his own. She would draw him into the bosom of a riotous professional family to replace the one he'd lost.

The Barrymores

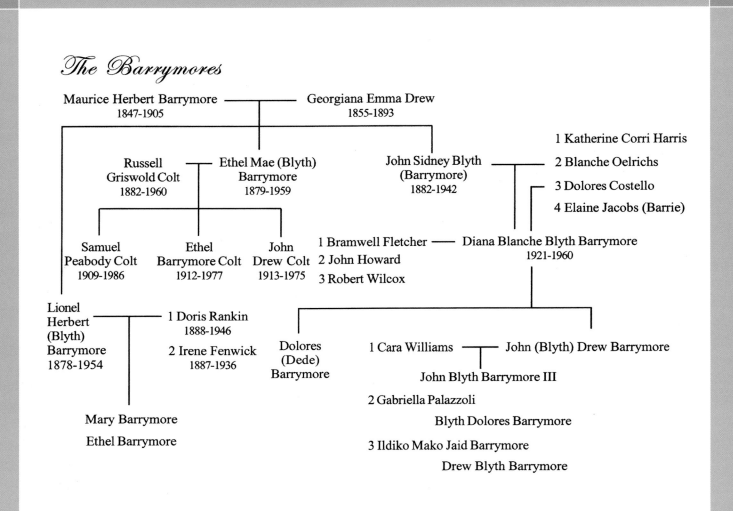

Maurice Herbert Barrymore ——— Georgiana Emma Drew
1847-1905   1855-1893

Russell ― Ethel Mae (Blyth)   John Sidney Blyth   1 Katherine Corri Harris
Griswold Colt   Barrymore   (Barrymore)   2 Blanche Oelrichs
1882-1960   1879-1959   1882-1942   3 Dolores Costello
                                                                4 Elaine Jacobs (Barrie)

Samuel   Ethel   John   1 Bramwell Fletcher ——— Diana Blanche Blyth Barrymore
Peabody Colt   Barrymore Colt Drew Colt   2 John Howard   1921-1960
1909-1986   1912-1977   1913-1975   3 Robert Wilcox

Lionel
Herbert   ― 1 Doris Rankin
(Blyth)   1888-1946
Barrymore
1878-1954   2 Irene Fenwick   Dolores   1 Cara Williams ——— John (Blyth) Drew Barrymore
                  1887-1936   (Dede)
                                    Barrymore   John Blyth Barrymore III

                                              2 Gabriella Palazzoli
Mary Barrymore   Blyth Dolores Barrymore

Ethel Barrymore   3 Ildiko Mako Jaid Barrymore
                                                    Drew Blyth Barrymore

The First Barrymores

It is legend that when two members of the family gather together, there is the theater.

—DRAMA CRITIC JOHN ANDERSON

BARRY HAD BEEN GIVEN the role of leading man in Augustin Daly's touring company with Georgie playing opposite him. They enhanced each other on and off the stage, and Barry was idyllically happy with the arrangement. They played through the New York boroughs to much acclaim, and people clamored to see the handsome couple who seemed so right for each other. Barry was earning a salary that allowed him to become his own man, which he found much more to his liking than sheltering under the roofs of relatives.

By now Barry was the undisputed king of the matinees. Actresses, matinee girls, working women, even charwomen, agreed that no handsomer man had ever tread the boards of Broadway. Even men had to admit that there had never been a more impressive specimen of nineteenth-century manhood. (Indeed, at the time Jack Barrymore's career was winding down, people were still discussing whether he or his sire was better looking.) Theaters that sold Barry's photographs could not keep them in stock. Women put his picture in their lockets, on their vanity mirrors, in scrapbooks and diaries.

As always, accusations of laziness, or lack of motivation, followed Barry. Here was a man who cared as much for his life outside the theater as he did for the fictional one he played on stage, and critics could not forgive him

for giving less than all of himself to every performance. "There is no man on the American stage to-day who can play the melodramatic hero better than he if he wants to," wrote one critic of the period. "When one knows what a really brilliant man Maurice Barrymore is, how far ahead he is in talent of most of the successful actors on our boards, one feels inclined to kick him as he shambles through his part." He would never escape such criticisms, but then he didn't often read his own reviews.

In September 1877, Augustin Daly closed the Fifth Avenue Theater after losing money steadily for several productions, and his players went on to other companies. Lester Wallack offered Maurice double what he was making with Daly, but out of loyalty to Daly, Maurice agreed to go on the road with him, as did his brother-in-law Jack Drew. Georgie went home to Philadelphia to await the birth of the first Barrymore heir.

Audiences didn't respond much better to the touring company than they had to the performances at the Fifth Avenue. Fortunately for the Barrymores, Barry had come into some money. His older brother, Will, had purchased his interest in the New Zealand property left to them by their father, and Barry's windfall amounted to around seven thousand dollars. A short while after Lionel was born April 12, 1878, Barry decided to invest part of his inheritance. He had already been working on a play he called *A Bitter Expiation,* a dark Russian melodrama. When leading man Henry Montague died of consumption while touring Sardou's *Diplomacy,* Barry was contracted to finish the tour. When he saw how receptive Chicago was to the production and learned that the manager planned to close regardless of the interest, Barry used a part of his inheritance to buy the U.S. and Canadian touring rights to the play. Barry's old London friend Frederick B. Warde, who had been touring with *Diplomacy,* joined him to form the Warde and Barrymore Combination.

The two new managers engaged staff and company immediately. Signor and Madame Majeroni from Italy were signed for the key roles of Count Orloff and Countess Zicka. The tour turned out to be a family affair. Jack Drew, Mrs. Drew's best friend, Alexina Fisher Baker, Annie Edmonson Warde (Frederick's wife), and Georgie Drew Barrymore were among the players. Reviews were good, and Barrymore and Warde had every reason to expect success until their business agent enraged the Majeronis by cutting their salaries, then absconded with Barry's production funds. After that the production seemed cursed. Illness disrupted the company, and attendance at performances was poor.

The partners decided to split into two companies, covering twice as much territory, giving twice as many performances. "As the venture was not proving profitable, Warde and Barrymore, a short time after we had gone on tour, decided to split. Warde was to take part of the company and go West. Barrymore was to keep some of the actors, engage additional talent, and play the Southern territory," Jack Drew wrote. Barry went back to Philadelphia to plan a tour to begin in January. He engaged Jack Drew, Alexina Fisher Baker, R. Rees Davis, and Benjamin C. Porter, an actor he knew from Boston. Alexina's daughter, Josephine, was called in to take Georgie's part because she was pregnant again.

The tour was not profitable, but it was fortunate for Jack Drew. He courted Josephine Baker throughout the tour, much to her mother's delight. To have her daughter fall in love with the son of her dearest friend was a dream come true. And Jack and Josephine weren't the only victims of Cupid. After sitting up late nights over coffee with Ellen Cummins, who had the role of Countess Zicka, Ben Porter proposed to her. But their wedding would never take place.

"It was on this tour—at Marshall, Texas—that Ben Porter was killed and Barrymore severely wounded," Jack Drew wrote. "We had played at the Opera House that night in March, the sixth anniversary of my appearance on the stage, and were waiting for a train to take us to Texarkana." Since Jack was not an eyewitness to the shooting itself, we must assume that he heard some of the following details from Barry.

> We were stopping at the Station Hotel, and most of us went there directly after the play; but Barrymore, Porter and Miss Cummins decided to have something to eat, and they went to the only lunch room that was open, the one at the station.
>
> This lunch room was a sort of bar as well. One man was waiting on both parts of the room. A man named Jim Curry, an employee of the railroad and a deputy sheriff, began using offensive language and affronted Miss Cummins.
>
> Barrymore demanded that he stop.
>
> "I can do any of you up," said Curry.
>
> "I suppose you could," answered Barrymore, "with your pistol or knife."
>
> "I haven't got any pistol or knife. I'll do it with my bunch of fives," said Curry, as he proudly displayed a fist like a sledge hammer.
>
> "Then," said Barrymore, throwing off his coat, "I'll have a go at you."
>
> But Curry did have a gun and he shot Barrymore, wounding him in the shoulder. When Porter rushed to Barrymore's aid, Curry shot him. Porter died almost immediately, on the station platform.

JACK DREW WAS ALERTED by the gunshots and "ran along the station platform and entered the only place that was lighted, the lunch room. As I entered, the man with the gun grabbed me. Why he did not shoot I do not know. In another minute or two the sheriff of Marshall arrived, took the gun away from his deputy and locked him up." The troupe stayed in Marshall until Barry was able to travel. "When the physician showed him the ball that had been cut out of the muscle of his back, Barrymore said: 'I'll give it to my son Lionel to cut his teeth on.'"

The troupe returned to Philadelphia broke but unbowed. Louisa was unsympathetic to her son-in-law's misfortunes, considering him to be merely the victim of a barroom brawl. Barry never did see justice done, though he traveled to Marshall twice for that purpose. On the second visit he was sitting on the station platform where his friend Porter had died, waiting for the train to arrive, when, according to Jack Drew, Curry's lawyer came out and stood in the light from the door and asked: "Is Maurice Barrymore here?" Barrymore, who noticed that the lawyer had his hand on his hip pocket, declared himself present a little reluctantly. He thought that there might be another shooting imminent.

"Here," said the lawyer, taking his gun from his pocket and holding the butt out to Barrymore, "is the pistol that killed Porter and wounded you."

Barrymore took it, thanked the lawyer, examined the gun gingerly and handed it back.

JACK DREW RECOUNTED that "Curry was twice brought to trial, but acquitted. There were witnesses in court to testify that Curry had shot Porter and Barrymore in self-defense. As a matter of fact, at the time of the shooting there was no one in the lunch room except the participants and the man who was waiting upon them. He was spirited away and never appeared in court." Later they would learn that Curry was killed in another bar fight, some say shot in the face by an actor. Lionel said, "The story that I cut my teeth on a bullet extracted from my father's back is another of those figments about the Barrymores too happily told for me to deny at this date. I was one year old at the time, so the yarn is at least possible."

Lionel indicated that the adventures Barry faced did nothing to discourage him, even when he returned to Philadelphia without money and prospects. "These affairs never inhibited Mr. Barrymore's high-stepping spirits and good humors. If we were poor, we were poor, in a shabby-genteel kind of way. When we had money, when both Georgie and Maurice were gainfully employed on the stage, we children were handsomely turned out, had fine clothes, and considered ourselves rich. Most of the time we considered ourselves poor." The fact that neither Barry nor Georgie were good financial managers ensured that the family would be poor when they weren't weren't working, for they did not often put money away for rainy days.

When Barry walked out on the stage the first time after the shooting, he was met with a standing ovation. His popularity as a matinee idol was at an all-time high, but he was in search of more than admiration for his handsome face and his ability to portray fictional characters. He wanted to go beyond the stage and become an acknowledged playwright. While he was recovering from his gunshot wound, he had been polishing up his new play, *The Debt of Honor.* Wallack had agreed to produce it the following season.

Barry's dream was not to be realized with *The Debt of Honor,* a translation of a French drama. A play based on the same source opened at the Park Theater in New York, and Wallack decided not to produce Barry's play because it was so similar. The hopeful playwright sent a copy of the play to John Clayton, an old friend in London, a masterful actor who planned to prove himself as manager of the Royal Court Theater the following season.

That season Barry toured in *The Rivals* with his mother-in-law. Georgie traveled with the Gosche-Hopper troupe—a company headed by DeWolf Hopper, a young man with an inheritance and little experience who had offered Georgie a good salary so that his production would have "a name." (Much later Hopper would marry chorus girl Elda Furry, who would become the most powerful woman in Hollywood—gossip columnist Hedda Hopper.) Georgie committed to the production for $125 a week, money that was needed in the Barrymore house at that time. In the bargain, the care of the child actress traveling with the company fell to her.

On the way to play in Mobile, Alabama, the train conveying the Gosche-Hopper players crashed headlong into a freight train being piloted by a drunken crew. Georgie and her little charge were thrown the length of the sleeping car. Most of the crew were injured or killed, and the actors worked as nurses and rescue workers. Georgie used her fur piece to pillow the head of a dying fireman.

When he next returned to Philadelphia, news awaited Barry that Clayton in London wished to produce *The Debt of Honor.* Contracts were enclosed. A few small rewrites were suggested. Barry did not want to leave those revisions to another writer, so he made plans to sail for England, even though Clayton was not overjoyed to learn of his plans.

Georgie was in no position to join Barry on his trip. Lionel was three years old and Ethel was almost two. Georgie was pregnant again, and she was still committed for another season to her engagement in *One Hundred Wives* for Hopper. So, at the age of thirty-nine, dapper and successful, Barry returned alone to London, the place of his youth.

He was welcomed and celebrated. He had not seen London for a decade, but it did not seem to have changed much, except that Ned Donnelly's beloved sport had become legitimate, and he had become the director of the University of British Boxing. Barry fell effortlessly into a bachelor routine. He sparred and worked out daily, and he made the revisions Clayton requested. Squire Bancroft and his wife invited Barry to join them at the Theater

Georgiana Drew Barrymore with her children, Ethel, Lionel, and Jack. When Ethel's three children were small, she had a portrait made that recalled this childhood moment.

Royal Haymarket, which would have been a flattering, tempting offer, had it come at another time. Significantly, during his stay in London he met Madame Helena Modjeska and became hypnotized by her, and she by him. She would play a large role in Barry and Georgie's life very soon. When there was nothing further for him to do on the play and he had reassured himself that John Clayton was not going to ruin his work, Barry returned to Philadelphia.

AFTER THE BIRTHS OF Lionel, Ethel, and John, Barry and Georgie played to audiences all over the country. The children occasionally traveled with their parents, but usually they stayed in Philadelphia with "Mummum" (Mrs. Drew), "Aunt Tibby" (Aline Stephens), and "Uncle Googan" (Sidney Drew), and the help in the "white-shuttered, white-stepped row house" into which Louisa had moved the family after the death of John Drew Sr. As Barry and Georgie traveled extensively, together and apart,

Louisa Drew was the source of stability in the lives of the Barrymore children.

Mummum was steadfast and unchanging. She had her rules and her opinions, and she expressed herself without hesitation. She followed the same routine for thirty years. Though she disguised her kind heart under a gruff exterior, she gave generously to her family without regret. She was not warm in the traditional sense, and Ethel as a child found her frightening, but little Jack at least found her caring and tender in a distant way.

To the Barrymore children, their witty, attractive parents were beautiful strangers, mysterious and admired but not really known. They brought glamour and high society into Mrs. Drew's house, but they could often be distant and sometimes intimidating. Though the children had a great affection for these transient people and their beauty and poise, they never really knew them as they did Mummum. As adults, they would be reduced to quoting stories they had heard from other people because they were left with so few actual memories themselves of their parents.

Barry dressed impeccably on stage, but off stage his costumes were comical and sometimes even bizarre.

EVEN THOUGH HIS parental concern was somewhat casual, Barry was revered by his young sons. "He was at all times an amusing person," Lionel wrote. He "had read everything in the world, in French and English, and he liked children. He romped and roared with Jack and me, usually at late hours when Mummum would get annoyed, and he told us outrageous stories of derring-do, blood and thunder. He recited spates of Shakespeare on occasion with leers and winks—perhaps, who knows, influencing the taste of his sons."

And Barry knew everyone. His children were introduced to luminaries on both sides of the Atlantic. Ethel remembered one of the only times she was punished—when she screamed and ran away from the visage of Oscar Wilde while she was supposed to be serving him dainties from a tray. Lionel recounted a boyhood trip to New York and his first encounter with Mark Twain.

This came about when Maurice Barrymore was playing in *Captain Swift* at the Madison Theater. During one of my holidays I accompanied him to the Hoffman House, one of his favorite places to hold forth. A bushy gentleman entered and ordered a hot apple toddy.

It is an aromatic wonderful drink, very solacing, they say. Mark Twain had one of these. My father took me by the hand and introduced me. He knew Mark Twain well, as indeed he knew all of the great people of the day. He introduced him correctly, of course, as Mr .Clemens. . . . "This is Mr. Clemens, Lionel," he said. "But I expect you know him as Mark Twain." I did indeed. We were old friends and had mutual acquaintances in Tom Sawyer and Huckleberry Finn. So I looked Mark Twain in the eye then and began telling him his own story, the part about Nigger Jim, and I gave it to him verbatim, mostly whole paragraphs at a time, except for some interpolations of my own which seemed to improve the tale. My father tried kicking me under the table to stop me from this impertinence of reciting Mark Twain's own story back to him, but Mr. Clemens laid a hand on his arm and gave me his whole attention. At the end of my recital there were tears in his eyes. He beckoned a waiter and bought me an apple with spice and hot water, omitting of course, the brandy. I was highly pleased with myself, unaware that I had pulled a potwalloping enormity.

"I SAW MARK TWAIN often after that," Lionel wrote, "but this was the main time."

Barry once took Jack to dine with Buffalo Bill and his press agent. In the atmosphere of the New York restaurant Cody's long hair looked effeminate to Jack, and he kept grinning impishly and threatening to laugh out loud. When Barry finally understood his son's behavior, he dragged him off to the washroom and gave him a dressing down. "You'd better be careful," Barry told his youngest son. "He'll carve your heart out." Jack had no trouble keeping his face straight for the remainder of the meal.

Barry knew artists, writers, and musicians. When he was in the mood to entertain his sons, he might take them to any number of studios, salons, theaters, gyms, and bar-rooms. During his rounds Barry encountered people who were so thrilled with his wit that they would preserve his words for the ages. Anyone fortunate enough to have even a minor conversation with Barry came away with some-thing to save; they wrote and retold the stories. "Maurice used to say things that amused people but puzzled them afterwards," Lionel wrote. "Once, I recall, a man asked him what another man was like. My father took this under consideration, thought about it, cocked an eye, rubbed his nose, and delivered a solemn opinion. "'I'll tell you,'" he said, "'He looks like someone who might play the piano.'"

Early in her career Marie Dressler played Cunigonde in Barry's *Waldemar, The Robber of the Rhine*. Dressler hated the part of the comic robber; she wanted to become a brilliant tragedienne. "You were born to make people laugh," Barry told her gently. He realized that she was longing to be taken seriously in the great roles, to move audiences to tears. "Don't fly in the face of fate," he told the large, determined actress. She took his advice, and her comedic talents eventually won her an Academy Award.

George LeBrun, who would later become head of the New York Board of Coroners, worked as cashier at the Albemarle Café at Broadway and Twenty-fourth Street while he was going to school. He was another person who

would forever remember Barry. "During the 1880s this café was a favorite meeting place for actors, writers and men about town," LeBrun wrote. "It was there that I met Maurice Barrymore. One night I entertained a group of the actors by giving an impersonation of Henry Irving singing 'It's English You Know,' and Maurice Barrymore clapped me on the back and urged me to go on the stage." LeBrun wrote this in 1962—at the age of one hundred! How charming and memorable Maurice must have been to have come to LeBrun's mind *eighty years* after the chance encounter while he was organizing a century of memories into 245 pages.

"And he wrote plays," Lionel noted with pride. "These included *Bitter Expiation* in 1880, *Honor* in 1881, *Homeward Bound* (with Julian Magnus) in 1882, a comic opera *The Robber of the Rhine* with music by Charles Puerner, in 1892, and most importantly, *Najezda. Najezda* was first produced in San Francisco with Madame Modjeska as the star and George Osborne as the equiva-lent of Baron Scarpia. Maurice and Modjeska played it in the East in 1884, including New York and Baltimore, my father took it to London in 1886 and played at the Haymarket with Emily Rigl."

On that trip to London, the whole family came along, and they stayed for two years. "Everything about those two years was magical," Ethel recalled. But that was after a sur-realistic tour that included Barry, an amorous Madame Mojeska, her jealous husband, Barry's suspicious wife, and their three children. Georgie and Lionel were pressed into service at various performances because of illness or attri-tion. Georgie, realizing that the leading lady had more than a professional interest in her husband, interfered with Mojeska's plans for Barry at every opportunity. Eventually Georgie developed warm feelings for Modjeska, and the actress would be responsible for Georgie's conver-sion to Catholicism.

While he toured with Modjeska, Barry revised *A Bitter Expiation* into his masterpiece, *Najezda*. Madame Mojeska agreed to play the lead in the new play "to give it a start," if Barry would play opposite her. Barry found himself performing in a play in which he had written a strong part for his paramour, and another one for his wife. As often happened with Barry, his charm got him through the period unscathed.

WHILE THEY WERE in London, an elegant dinner party was given at the Grand Café Royale, and Barry and

The first great Barrymore profile. Barry was sometimes called "the Bedouin of Broadway."

Maurice did not have his sons' aversion to playing perfumed and bewigged lovers.

Georgie were seated with Emily Rigl (one of Barry's old flames), Oscar Wilde, Sarah Bernhardt, Bernhard's manager Henry E. Abbey, and actress Lillie Langtry. There could not have been a greater gathering of loveliness in the world of the theater, and Georgie shone brightly among them. During the evening full of wit and grand repartee, the celebrated Sarah jousted verbally with Barry in English and in French. Barry responded to one of Bernhardt's jabs with a claim that he had attended school with Miss Bernhardt's son, an allusion to the fact that she was a number of years older than Barry. The exchange lost its humor for the actress, but Barry, who never meant to wound with his wit, noticed nothing. The following day he sent the French translation of his beloved *Najezda* to Madame Bernhardt.

"She kept *Najezda* for two years and returned it with scant thanks and no comment," Lionel wrote.

"Immediately thereafter, *Tosca* came out and it was Maurice's play. There was no question about it. It was an open-and-shut case of plagiarism." Barry was astounded. Word of Bernhardt's reaction to his righteous indignation made its way back to him. "She struck a pose. She flicked a hand in lofty dismissal and said: 'If a great man gets the germ of an idea from some—some obscure American, what does it matter? These things often happen.'" Lionel was impressed with Barry's retort. "A man is no less a thief who steals from his own hat rack my walking stick, where I have confidently placed it, and builds an umbrella on it," Barry said. Bernhardt felt no obligation to dignify his accusation with a response.

Perhaps if Barry had thought a little more about the possible results of offending the lady at the elegant dinner party, he would not have sent her his beloved *Najezda*.

"Later, Puccini wrote the music for the opera *La Tosca*, from a plot based on the play by Sardou—whose inspiration was plainly *Najezda*," Lionel recalled. "Many years later I met the gentleman, at about the time when he was writing *The Girl of the Golden West*. He sat at a table in the dining room of the Knickerbocker Hotel in New York one evening with David Belasco, John Williams, and John Luthor Long. I approached, and as I did, I could hear Belasco whisper to Puccini: 'Watch out, here it comes!' But, I merely bowed and said: 'Might it be that I could shake the hand of the maestro?' And I was allowed to shake the hand of the maestro." What emotion he felt and did not reveal at the time of that handshake, Lionel left to his readers' imaginations. "Still, whenever I hear *La Tosca* played, I experience venal emotions," he wrote. "I believe that I should get a rake off for my father's plot." Bernhardt broke Barry's heart, and he never quite recovered from the blow. He was in his mid-forties when his life began to slide downhill.

ETHEL RECALLED HER grandmother as a "regal presence," and Lionel wrote that "what security the young Barrymores could lay claim to resided in Mrs. John Drew." Louisa had a special tenderness for her grandson Jack Barrymore, the baby of Barry and Georgie's brood. Whenever she could arrange it she kept Jack with her. Jack would, in turn, love his Mummum without reserve. "To my mind," he said, "my grandmother typified everything that an actress should be." Despite her feelings for Jack, Louisa tried never to allow her younger grandson to take advantage of any sentiment on her part.

Ethel related a story that revealed Mrs. Drew's approach to her grandson's tricks. One day Jack was late for a meal. In hopes that his tardiness would not be noticed, or at least not punished, he rushed in, out of breath, and with a trembling, excited voice, he asked his grandmother, "Mummum, have you ever seen a house all painted black?"

"No," she said. "Nor have you. Now sit down."

Louisa often had her hands full with Jack, and when she wasn't amused by his antics she did not hesitate to punish him with her old worn slipper. He stole her jewelry and secreted it in the attic; while a policeman was investigating, Louisa read Jack's face and deduced where her gems could be found. He drank all the wine left in the glasses after one of his grandmother's dinner parties and passed out cold. The doctor needed only one look to deduce what ailed the child.

Throughout his life, older, motherly women would protect and nurture Jack, and he would establish lasting relationships with some of them, such as Sister Vincent, who taught at the "little boy's school" he attended; the landlady in New York who allowed him to turn her upper apartment into a haven for bachelors; and Mae Costello, who eventually became his third mother-in-law. These associations appealed to Jack because of the warm, comfortable relationship he had with his grandmother.

IN 1889, MAURICE decided to move his family to New York, closer to their work and his entertainment. Jack was seven, Ethel was ten, and Lionel was eleven. The population of Manhattan at that time was approximately one-and-a-half million, just a small town compared to today's standards. For a short time the Barrymores took up residence at 1564 Broadway on a plot of land that would later be the site of the Palace Theater.

They all looked forward to seeing Uncle Jack and Aunt "Dodo" more frequently than before. Jack Drew was the toast of the town at that time—it was said that people went to the theater to learn from Drew how to behave and what to wear. People strolled for enjoyment, everyone in finest attire, hoping to see and be seen on Broadway, and they wanted to be in style. With their admired and adored parents, who knew everyone and were known in return, the young Barrymore children were at the heart of the excitement.

In the summer, Barry loved to visit the zoo. He would take the boys along on a witty tour of the wildlife, allowing them to crawl into animal cages and get as filthy with dirt and droppings as they wanted. Barry entranced them with his knowledge of animal lore and behavior. His lectures drew passersby who appreciated not only the information but also the colorful manner of his delivery.

One of Barry's most endearing qualities was the way he had with animals. Since his young days in India, he had never met a four-footed creature he didn't like. He teased his children that they were odd because their father had been raised on goat's milk. From the time he was old enough to be outdoors, he had collected stray animals and tamed wild ones. His first heart-wrenching pain, at age eleven, occurred when his father announced that his dog Rahj was not going to England for schooling with him. As soon as he left Oxford and moved into lodgings where he could keep a pet, Barry acquired another dog

Barry in *Captain Swift,* a role that allowed him to swagger.

and named him Rahj II. His friend Paul Potter talked him out of taking Rahj II on his first acting tour, saying that the life of a traveling player was no life for a dog.

When Georgie and Barry traveled, he would often have to dash around the city before the trip boarding and adopting out monkeys, dogs, and birds. He had been known to quarrel with landladies over beavers and rabbits. Amy Leslie, drama critic for the *Chicago News,* said, "He is a rather irrational and eccentric lover of animals," and that comment is kind. Apparently he had a hard time passing up ownership of any unusual creature, no matter how many he already had or whether the owner was asking a ridiculous price. "When his dogs, birds, beavers, cats, rabbits, and weird furry cubs of various paternity accumulated beyond endurance of his housemates he bought a farm and kept his menagerie there," wrote biographer

James Kotsilibas-Davis. Barry would use his ramshackle farm as a refuge for himself and a way station for his boys when necessary.

When the Barrymores rented an apartment in New York, Georgie furnished the new place with her money, and Barry contributed a trunk of books and a pedigreed Clydesdale terrier named Belle of Clyde. Barry took Belle everywhere with him. When he was on tour, he brushed and groomed the dog's silky, easily tangled coat faithfully for an hour every morning.

Barry returned from one tour with a bear cub that thrilled his two sons. When Georgie saw it, she began to cry, not because of the bear but because Barry had returned from Kansas City with no money in his pockets, though money was the reason he was touring. The bear had to be taken to the zoo soon after.

At the World's Columbian Exposition of 1893 in Chicago, Barry fell in love with a pair of skunks he purchased from their owner even though he quoted an exorbitant price. Barry named his new pets Minnehaha and Molly Brown and left the fair happy, a skunk tucked in either pocket of his overcoat. Within days they responded only to Barry and were given the run of the train.

His love of animals got out of hand on his *Aristocracy* tour for Charles Frohman. Barry's constant animal companions inspired other players to bring their pets along on the train. When they arrived in San Francisco, the hotel allowed Barry to room with Belle and the two skunks, but when he went to the docks and purchased several rare dogs from Japan, he was asked to leave. For a while, he was forced to house his animals in his dressing room, which left little space for him. He rented rooms in boardinghouses and left the Japanese dogs there while he worked. When he was able to return for them, he had forgotten the address of the house and was forced to go door to door until he located the room and the dogs.

When the *Aristocracy* company left for Los Angeles, several other actors had added animals of their own. Bruce McRae had taken a liking to two prairie dogs and a pair of Japanese mice (Waldemar and Hildegard), and Barry wasn't yet finished acquiring foreign livestock either. When the company passed through San Francisco again, Barry came back from the docks with a large cage full of red-headed birds. He tried to borrow enough money to buy an anteater, but he found no one willing to contribute. Word of Mr. Barrymore's love of exotic animals spread up and down the coast. At many of the stations they pulled into, they would see people with cages waiting on the platform. "Mr. Barrymore!" they would call, trying to interest the eccentric actor in unusual or superior specimens. At one stop he begged his colleagues for loans to purchase a chimpanzee. That scheme worked out no better than his pleas for the price of an anteater. He did secure a loan for the male half of a beautiful pair of Huskies, and the following pay day he sent for the female partner. Why he wanted the dogs is a mystery, as he already had four Huskies that had been on Commander Peary's arctic expedition, which Peary had personally sent to Barry as a gift. On his farm he also had about thirty offspring of those four original dogs.

Barry purchased Bruno the bear from a circus animal trainer for ten dollars. The bear could catch beer bottles that were tossed to him, tear off the bottlecaps with his teeth, and down the beer in one swallow. The bear might have been the only creature who had no regard for Barry's skill with animals. After he wrecked a hotel room, tearful Barry was forced to return him. Barry was so distraught that the animal handler promised to send him a pair of beavers to cheer him up.

As soon as Barry arrived in a new location he would load his pets on a carriage and go in search of a lenient landlord who didn't mind animals sleeping inside and who had room in back for the others. His fellow actors laughed to see him drive away, cages piled helter skelter in and on top of the carriage, and he was often late for rehearsals because he had to travel so far to the theater.

Finally, the train hands began to complain about the animals. The sleeping berths and baggage car were full of creatures, not all of them friendly. The crew was being forced to make unscheduled stops to take care of the needs of the animals, and they were tired of the actors' assurances. Eventually they solved the problem for themselves by removing the baggage car from the train, leaving nowhere for the animals to ride. The company had to load themselves and their animals into a boat and sail up the coast to Tacoma, Washington, because they could find no train to carry them to their next engagement. Barry finally retired from *Aristocracy* in a huff when Frohman announced a schedule of one night stands and Barry found it impossible to travel with eleven dogs, two skunks, various rodents, and at least thirty-five small red-headed Japanese birds.

While Barry toured with Olga Nethersole in *The Lady of the Camellias,* he gathered several monkeys, a number of birds, a mongoose, and a racoon. Barry was supposed to be traveling with the Columbia Theatre Stock Company as leading man when his dilapidated farm burned to the ground and only a few of his animals survived. He was devastated and could not function at all for several days. His friends were shocked at his unshaven appearance and glassy eyes. He clung to his Belle of Clyde after that and even began to allow the dog to go on stage with him. She would lie at his feet or on a rug, upstaging no one, asking for no reward but his presence.

When Belle died at the age of seven years, Barry went on a two-day drunk. The pain of the loss stayed with him, and he invented a fantasy dog he claimed to lead on a leash of glass. That fantasy offered him no solace and concerned his friends, so he acquired a Maltese cat named Patrick Boniface, who was not meant to replace his dear Belle but only to take his mind off of her.

Barry's eccentricity about animals inspired Mrs. Fiske to

action. While they were touring in *Becky Sharpe,* she began to take in stray animals, nurse them back to health, and find good homes for them.

Barry would pass this uncanny ability to communicate with animals on to his sons, particularly Jack, who would throughout his life collect unusual pets.

MAURICE BARRYMORE WAS the shining star among many stars at the Lambs Club, where critics and reviewers were not allowed and men of art felt free to pontificate. There were times he would take his young son Jack along with him and check him in the cloakroom to sleep through the revelries, debating, and exchange of witticisms.

In 1892, Louisa closed out her business with the Arch Street Theater. She was no longer making money and she wasn't happy with the change from stock companies to visiting stars that was taking place in the world of theater. Her run in Sheridan's *The Rivals* with Joseph Jefferson was over after twelve seasons. She was seventy-two years old.

She closed up the house in Philadelphia and moved to New York, where she stayed either with John Drew and his wife Josephine or Sidney Drew and his wife Gladys. Sidney arranged work for his mother because when she wasn't working she was unhappy and restless.

I was a quiet kid who could be left alone for as many hours as our guardians desired if they put a paintbox in my hands. And there was Uncle Googan.

"Uncle Googan was Sidney Drew," Lionel wrote. The mystery of Sidney's birth parents persists to this day, though Lionel believed he knew the answer—or part of it. "In her autobiography, published in 1899, Louisa Lane Drew states that she had adopted Sidney. Mrs. Drew, of course, may say what she wished in the matter, but Uncle Googan certainly looked like her." At any rate, this was an engaging fellow who seemed at all times to have a deal more Barrymore than Drew in him. He did work all the time, being afflicted with the usual occupational hazard of actors, and was frequently told off as baby sitter for his young niece and nephews. On such occasions, Uncle Googan would march us sedately down Chestnut Street, a model of avuncular correctness, turn sharp right, and repair some blocks away to a pool hall.

The children always answered yes when asked if they would like to watch their uncle "hit the pretty balls." And "Uncle Googan could hit the pretty balls masterfully," Lionel recalled. "Indeed, Uncle Googan

was a shark. It was his habit to lie in wait for suckers, engage them in contest after having convinced them that he was a feeble tyro, raise the ante, and relieve them in the last game of as much folding money as possible." Uncle Googan livened the house with his gaiety and general naughtiness. He brought home women his mother thought weren't good enough for him and eventually married Gladys Rankin, the daughter of Mckee Rankin and Kitty Blanchard, very successful actors. Among their most famous performances was *The Danites in the Sierras,* written by Joaquin Miller, which they played on tour in the U.S. and London. Mrs. Drew approved of the union. Perhaps she was reminded of herself by her impervious new daughter-in-law, who seemed able to keep Sidney in line.

During the season, when Georgie was playing in New York City, Ethel anticipated Sundays, when her mother would usually be at home. Georgie lifted the spirits of the household. She made everybody laugh and filled the house with merriment. Her wit was renowned, and no one could get the best of her quick tongue—not even Maurice. Ethel reveled in her mother's presence, but they remained strangers. Drews never had revealed their feelings easily, and nothing about that was likely to change.

Other people told Ethel about her mother. Charles Frohman related how Georgie had telegraphed him to ask for new clothes for a play she was touring. Frohman cabled back, "No." Georgie received that response. "Oh," was the answer she sent. The exchange delighted the theatrical manager, and Georgie got her new clothes.

Georgie had become ill on tour in *Wilkerson's Widows,* and she was given doctor's orders for rest and quiet. She decided to sail to the Bahamas. The day she left, the gravity of the situation struck Maurice, who cried as he held her hand before she boarded the ship. No one said anything to the children about how sick their mother was.

While Georgie was away, the boys were staying at the old farm Maurice owned on Staten Island, where they were watched over by Edward Briggs, the farm's tenant, who was referred to as the "Black Prince." Edward fed the animals and allowed the boys to do as they pleased. The thirty or more dogs had the run of the place, as Maurice had decreed, and the boys slept and ate with them. When Louisa heard of the situation, she sent a train ticket to young Jack and commanded that he join her at her summer residence. Lionel was left with the Prince.

When Georgie returned from the Islands, she felt somewhat better. As soon as she returned to work, however, she once again collapsed. She was diagnosed with bronchitis and was advised to go west for the weather. She chose Santa Barbara. Ethel was summoned to accompany her mother because other family members were engaged for the season. Mrs. Drew was in Boston, Maurice was on tour, and John Drew was in Europe. John and Lionel were at Seton Hall.

Ethel met Georgie in New York. They cruised down to Panama, crossed it by train, then sailed up the coast to Mexico and then to California. Ethel was excited on the trip and nervous about pleasing her beautiful mother. She suspected her mother was very ill, though she did not let herself acknowledge it. "It was bad just before the boat sailed when Mamma was saying good-bye to Papa and begging him not to forget her. It was my first sight of tragedy, although I didn't know it then," she wrote.

Georgie was clearly very ill. Though she tried to hide her fears from her thirteen-year-old daughter, Ethel heard her at night asking herself, "What will become of my poor kids?" Once again, the Drew upbringing led Ethel to hide from her mother the fact that she had heard. She was frightened but filled with hope as they settled down in "the lovely little house covered with roses even all over the roof and pouring into my window."

During their stay in Santa Barbara, the Barrymores were honored guests of the city, but Georgie's condition steadily deteriorated until one Sunday morning, when Ethel had left her mother in their rooms and walked to mass. On her way home the mayor's daughter rushed up to her and cried, "Oh Ethel, hurry home, your mother has had a hemorrhage!" Ethel got to her mother just before she died. Georgie didn't recognize her only daughter.

At the age of thirty four, Georgie Drew Barrymore passed away, leaving her thirteen-year-old daughter alone to arrange the details of her mother's funeral. Santa Barbara acquaintances were kind enough to help her send telegrams to Barry and Sidney Drew. They got word to the others, while Ethel dressed in a grown woman's black dress and pinned her hair up before calling on the undertaker. She arranged to accompany her mother's body back to Philadelphia, and she kept her chin up, showing no emotion, not even her fear, perhaps the best acting she had done in her life.

ETHEL WAS BACK at the Convent School a few months later when the mother superior showed her a newspaper clipping about her father. After Georgie's death, Barry

stayed away from the family. He mourned alone. He could not bear to return to the apartment he'd shared with his wife, so he moved into the Lambs' Club and set about to drown his sorrows. He gave away Georgie's belongings. Now, he had married Mamie Floyd, who as a child had had a crush on him. She was twenty-five years his junior. Many years would pass before Ethel came to terms with the news.

Lionel was scooped up by Louisa, who came to New York to take her grandson on tour with her. She felt that if he was no longer in school, then he had to work and work meant the stage. He was fifteen, and he had left school for the last time. Sidney Drew, the tour's manager, gave Lionel chores to do. He was an errand boy for his grandmother, who was perhaps the most famous actress on the American stage at the time.

Lionel had his first acting experience at New York's Fourteenth Street Theater on Christmas night, 1893, in *The Road to Ruin.* It was the sort of role in which an apprentice actor prayed he went unnoticed, and he did. Next, Mrs. Drew gave him the part of Thomas in *The Rivals,* the play in which she had become famous as Mrs. Malaprop. After the first performance in which he participated, Lionel received a note in his grandmother's familiar purple ink.

> My Dear Lionel:
>
> You must forgive me for not realizing that when Sheridan wrote the part of Thomas, he had a much older actor in mind. We feel that we were very remiss in not taking cognizance of this....We think, therefore, that the play as a whole would be bettered by the elimination of the front scene and have decided to do without it after this evening's performance. Sincerely and with deep affection,
>
> Your Grandmother,
> Mrs. Drew

The Barrymores are known for innovations they introduced to the entertainment industry. Perhaps this modification of Sheridan's play was Lionel's first big invention. "Since my debut," he wrote, "most performances of *The Rivals* have gone on without the front scene. I seem to have killed it for good. Or perhaps directors have been worried lest I come back and play the part again." Lionel was overjoyed to be fired. He could now return to nightly visits with Mrs. Drew without trepidation, enjoying cheese

Even though it was a small part, Lionel Barrymore studied with a real Italian organ grinder for his part in *The Mummy and the Hummingbird*. Some said he upstaged his famous uncle, John Drew, star of the play.

and crackers with her while she had her dram of rye whiskey before bedtime.

"What do you intend to try next?" she asked him that evening.

"Painting scenery," answered her older grandson.

"Your father was not such a distinguished actor either when he first started out," she replied.

For the next five years, until he was twenty, Lionel stayed in the company, performing bit parts, learning a craft that he always claimed he did not want to practice. After that, he enrolled in the Art Student's League in New York, where he studied for three years. He exhibited some talent, but life's realities began to intrude on the idyllic Bohemian atmosphere, and it became time for Lionel to go to work. That meant the stage, where he could find a regular paycheck. Actor and manager McKee Rankin came

to his aid and hired him to play whatever small parts he had. For many years Rankin had acted with his wife, Kitty Blanchard, a popular dancer and actress, in the stock company at the Philadelphia Arch Street Playhouse. They had three daughters, "Phyliss, who was married to the late Harry Davenport, Gladys, who became Mrs. Sidney Drew (Uncle Googan), and thus my aunt-by-marriage; and Doris. Doris became Mrs. Lionel Barrymore." At this point, Doris was a child and Lionel barely noticed her existence. One day, she would simply appear, sixteen years old and lovely, and Lionel would be captivated.

Mrs. Drew decided that Ethel should join her and Sidney in Montreal, and Ethel left the convent school for the last time. It was time to make her way in the world; she was fourteen years old, well past the age at which Mrs. Drew had been helping to support her family. The part of

Julia, which was given to Ethel for her debut in *The Rivals*, was a part that Joseph Jefferson usually chose to omit in his performances. It was included for Ethel as a favor to her grandmother. And so, without remembering ever being told "anything by anyone," Ethel began "an apprenticeship which was to last more than a half a century."

Only once did she dare ask Mummum about some aspect of acting. "She lifted her eyebrows and said, 'You should know that without being told,'" Ethel recalled.

After the run of *The Rivals* shut down, Ethel returned to New York to live with Mrs. Drew in John Drew's apartments. She was given a cheerless little room that matched her attitude at the time.

Ethel began looking for work and, as Lionel had found out, it was not always easy to come by, even for one from a family renowned on the stage. Ethel frequented the employment agencies looking for work. Mummum was no help, for she was disoriented herself, without work for the first time she could remember.

Though most of the Drews and the Barrymores were having trouble finding work, Jack Drew was now the brightest light on Broadway and his star continued to rise. "This was Uncle Jack's third year under the management of Charles Frohman, who had begun to institute the Star system in the American Theater with Uncle Jack as his first star," Ethel wrote. "Maude Adams, then Uncle Jack's leading lady, became Mr. Frohman's second star three years later in *The Little Minister*." Jack Drew had been a star when Frohman wined and dined and lured him away from Augustin Daly. By this time he was the stage's first superstar.

Though the Barrymores were an independent lot, Ethel finally appealed to Uncle Jack to help her find some work. She'd play maids or she'd be happy as an understudy. Uncle Jack came up with "a little tray carrying" in Frohman's company. "What I did then and during all three years with Uncle Jack was done in order to eat....I went on the stage because I did not know how to do anything but act—and I did not know how to do that."

But she *did* know how to do it. When the lead actress couldn't go on in *The Bauble Shop*, Ethel Barrymore, years younger than the lead and sizes smaller than the costumes, shone as Lady Kate Fennell. As Jack Drew had been in his first important role, Ethel was cool when she stepped on the stage. She gave no hint of nervousness or doubt. She did not have Mummum at her side as Uncle Jack had had during his first performance, but she did so well that she suffered a bitter shock to learn that she would not be given the part permanently. She had, however, caught the attention of Charles Frohman, who liked her for her similarities to her mother, whom he had loved.

Though Ethel was not a typical gallery girl, she developed a crush on William Gillette. He was playing at the time in *Secret Service*. "Fortunately for my young heart, he had matinees on days we didn't, and thus I was able to go every Thursday and rapturously admire him," she wrote. "I had his photograph—which I had bought—and hoped that someday I could have the thrill of meeting him." She would soon have that thrill and more.

After the New York run of *Rosemary*, in which Ethel had played a young maid, she went on tour with Uncle Jack Drew. One night in St. Louis, Jack summoned Ethel to his dressing room. "I have just had a most extraordinary telegram from C.F. about you," he told her. He handed the message to her and she read, "WOULD ETHEL LIKE TO GO TO LONDON WITH GILLETTE IN *SECRET SERVICE*?" Ethel certainly did want to go. "Why I didn't drop dead, I don't know," she recalled. "This great news was almost too much for me."

Everything Ethel owned fit into one small bag, so packing was short work. She picked up her ticket and made her way to the ship she'd been instructed to board. Her father had promised to see her off, after introducing her to Gillette. Ethel was used to being disappointed by Barry, so she thought little of the fact that he never showed up. A young actor of Ethel's acquaintance introduced her to the object of her crush. The leading man immediately took Ethel's hand and bowed. She felt a little disappointed meeting the man as opposed to her matinee idol.

She was not the least bit sorry to have accepted the engagement, however. Since the age of six, when she had lived with her parents in St. John's Wood, she had loved all things British because they reminded her of the happiest two years of her life. And now Ethel arrived in London the summer of Queen Victoria's Diamond Jubilee. She was enchanted by the celebrations to commemorate Her Majesty's sixtieth anniversary of rule. Ethel was impressed with the parade she watched from an acquaintance's parlor window. "I shall never forget the Indian princes, dripping from chin to waist with fabulous jewels, unbelievable strings of pearls, diamonds and rubies," she wrote. She was the darling of society. The Prince of Wales caught her performance the night she was called to leave her nurse role and take over the ingenue part. "I liked you so much better than the present girl," he said, and Ethel, delighted by his royal blue eyes, "fled, very happy and blushing

A young Jack Barrymore, who was already breaking
hearts on both coasts by the early 1900s.

A young Ethel Barrymore, who
inherited her grandmother's sense
of responsibility as well as her
incredible stage presence.

from head to foot." She was celebrated, entertained, and proposed to, but no one offered her a job.

When Ethel's money ran low, she booked passage back to America and announced her departure to her friends. But Lawrence Irving, Sir Henry Irving's serious, humorless son, had fallen in love with Ethel. He convinced his father to offer her a position with his company so she could stay near enough for him to convince her to marry him. Ellen Terry, Sir Henry's leading lady, agreed with the younger Irving, being a great matchmaker at heart.

Though Ethel was developing her own merits, Sir Henry's kindness came partly from his memories of Georgie Drew; he transferred his affection to her daughter, whom he found to possess some of the qualities he had so admired in the mother. When Ethel received word that her grandmother's health was failing, Irving gave her an advance on her pay so that she could hurry to her grandmother's side to say goodbye. Louisa Lane Drew was now seventy-seven years old. Her sons were on tours; Ethel and Lionel were, too. Young Jack Barrymore accompanied her to Larchmont, New York, where they took lodging in a boardinghouse by the sea. Though clearly in pain, she insisted that she was resting between engagements, which she had done every summer since she arrived on American shores.

Had Mummum known that she was spending her last days, she might not have changed anything. Jack was her favorite grandson, and she had tried to keep him by her side as much as she could throughout his sixteen years. The others didn't need her anymore—her sons were at the height of their fame, and Lionel and Ethel had begun their careers—only little Jack's future remained uncertain. Perhaps Louisa tried to influence Jack on those long days they sat in the sea breeze—Jack sketching landscapes and his grandmother pretending to read any number of paperback books she'd brought with her. No matter which one she picked up, she ended up with her finger stuck between the pages as a bookmark while she talked about the stage. Sometimes she shuffled the pages of her autobiography, adding details here and there.

Jack loved his grandmother without reservation, and he stayed at her side, though, as Lionel pointed out, at his age, growing tall and handsome, he could have found any number of "enterprises of his own which could have engaged him pleasantly." He did not. Every morning he assisted Mummum down the stairs, served her breakfast, and acted as errand boy, companion, and squire. Every evening he rubbed her feet, tucked her into bed, and sat by her side until she drifted off to sleep. Lionel wrote,

> With the death of Louisa Lane Drew, whose home had been the only home Ethel, Jack and I had ever known, our only link with stability and security disappeared. This was harder on Jack than on Ethel and me. Ethel had already arrived, was a celebrity and a star. I had been for some years on my own, but Jack had been Mummum's favorite, had lived with her and depended upon her. My mother and father, affectionate and generous persons though they certainly were, were actor and actress on the stage, traveling, living in hotels, spending money when they had it, mockingly enduring near-poverty when they didn't. The rearing of offspring was not their forte. They did what they could with what they had, which is all that anyone can ever do.

Barry, in a fit of paternal solicitude, took charge of Jack. He had been kicked out of his last school and was at loose ends after Mummum's death. When Barry and Mamie finished their vaudeville engagement playing *A Man of the World* at Proctors in New York, they sailed to England to do *The Heart of Maryland* with Jack in tow. Barry enrolled the boy in King's College School, where Jack set about immediately inventing reasons to leave school and visit London. He described a fictional "major" who often called for his immediate presence.

Barry saw his sister, Evelin Wace, whom he had not seen since as young Herbert Blyth he left Amritsar forty years before. After she was widowed in India she had brought her children to London to live. Their greetings were not particularly warm, but Ethel and Jack adored their new cousins and their Aunt Eva and spent quite a bit of time visiting them after Barry sailed back to America in July, leaving Jack in Ethel's care.

After breaking another heart or two—including one belonging to Winston Churchill—Ethel sailed for home. She left money with a friend to be doled out to Jack in small sums. The handsome boy fell into the same sporting life his father had led in London decades before. He was agile and fit, and he began to spar at the School of Arms. By the following fall, when Jack made it back to New York, he had learned to drink and swagger. He was clearly meant for the stage, but, as did his older brother Lionel, he did everything he could do to avoid his heritage.

The Great Barrymores

THE TIME HAD COME for the youngest Barrymore son to go to work. As Lionel had been, Jack was determined not to earn his living on the stage. He had a more noble calling—he wanted to be an artist, as Lionel also hoped to be. Jack had a dark artistic vision, which he believed stemmed from an event that happened when he was nine years old.

"I got into a fight with a schoolmate," John wrote, "and I threw a hard-boiled egg at him. I hit him right in the ear. It lodged there quite some time." One can almost imagine the smirk on Jack's face; the story, that egg hanging for a moment in the ear of his enemy, was still funny to him. Sister Vincent punished Jack by forcing him to contemplate a large copy of Dante's *Inferno*, which had been illustrated by Dore. "It opened up wide fields for me, things I had never dreamed of. It made such a lasting impression upon me that when I followed my own bent some years later and took up drawing, I tried to draw like Dore." Jack explained that he saw such nightmares in his head. He described his drawings as "steeped in gloom."

Jack drummed up a little art business through his association with Ethel. Charles Frohman paid him five dollars to design a poster for Francois Villon's *If I Were King*. At the last minute, Jack went to his art tutor Bridgeman and asked for help. Bridgeman erased and redrew and handed back a nicely rendered poster that Frohman would use for several years and resurrect when the play was rereleased. "I have no embarrassment in mentioning how good the drawing was," Jack wrote with tongue in cheek.

Jack also participated in an exhibition put on by the Press Artist's League, "a private affair run by a man who split with the artist if there was anything to split." He recalled "the thrill of seeing a sticker with the magic word 'sold' posted on a drawing." He wondered just who would have paid ten dollars for the work. "It wasn't a cheerful subject: a hangman is walking along a road, carrying a stick which casts a shadow behind him, and this is so cast that it suggests a gallows. Above the road, floating in the air, are the faces of men and women that the hangman has executed." Who was the collector who purchased the only Jack Barrymore drawing to be sold at an exhibit? "Andrew Carnegie had thought *The Hangman* worth ten dollars," Jack wrote. He had to split the income with the house, so five dollars was "the maximum recognition" he received for his drawing talents.

Ethel had dragged Jack home to America when she returned from her second summer in England, and she'd tried to keep an eye out for her brother. Eventually, he found a job in the art department at the New York *Evening Journal*. "During this time I did a variety of conventional

Ethel Barrymore in *Captain Jinks of the Horse Marines,* her first big role, for which she had special gowns designed by her father's friend Percy Anderson.

newspaper work, but usually my drawings illustrated something on the editorial page written by Arthur Brisbane," Jack wrote. Ethel was relieved that her younger brother had gainful employment. She had just been offered a part in Frohman's *Captain Jinks of the Horse Marines,* and she was throwing her soul into her first important part.

"The role was that of Madame Trentoni, very taxing for so young and inexperienced an actress. There was comedy, pathos and dancing in it. I was more worried about the dancing than about anything else," Ethel wrote. Among several beautiful costumes designed by Percy Anderson, she wore a long, tiered white dress sprinkled with silken roses that made women in the audience gasp when she came on stage, though "the notices were amazingly bad" at first. During this production Ethel developed the opening night anxiety that would stay with her for the rest of her life. It seems that when she became "important," she developed a sense of responsibility toward the entire company, and that responsibility filled her with dread lest she fail and in failing cause the entire company's downfall. But in *Captain Jinks* she did anything but fail. And she needn't have worried about the dancing either.

They opened at the Walnut Street Theater in Philadelphia, hometown of the Drew clan, where she was already passionately adored. Ethel got off to a bad start in front of her very friendly audience. Her voice did not carry when she offered her first line. "Speak up, Ethel," called an encouraging voice from the gallery. "You Drews is all good actors." That was enough to inspire Ethel.

Miss Ethel Barrymore had arrived; she would never again be anonymous. Lionel was studying painting and music, taking jobs on stage so that he could afford to pursue his passions. But Jack had not yet found his way. He lost his job at the *Evening Journal* because he cared nothing for deadlines and refused to make his drawings conform to the subject matter they were meant to illustrate. "You were an actor before you came here, weren't you?" Brisbane asked him. He suggested that Jack return to the stage post haste. "I didn't know whether I could or not, but I had to; so I did," Jack said, and he turned to the same person who had given Lionel his theatrical start—McKee Rankin.

JACK JOINED RANKIN in the Windy City. "Cleveland's, on Wabash Avenue, Chicago, had been converted into a theater overnight," Jack recalled about the location of his next acting effort. "Before McKee Rankin and a man

named Cleveland leased it for a season of the repertoire, with Nance O'Neil as the star, the building had been a cyclorama of the Battle of Gettysburg." The acoustics were poor and more like those in a warehouse than a theater. Jack's performances mirrored his surroundings and were "Simon-pure badness." In his role as Max in Sudernamm's *Magda,* he received notice in the local press. In the costume of a much larger German soldier, Jack was forced to use all the extra clothes the company could find to fill his double-breasted frock coat. The padding slipped gradually until the proud chest he had displayed in the first act had become a pot belly in the last. Amy Leslie, who had loved Jack's father and had reported in detail on his on and off stage activities, wrote, "Mr. John Barrymore…walked about the stage as if he had been all dressed up and forgotten."

Jack still maintained that he did not want to be an actor. "I was there merely because it was supposed that any member of a theater family ought to have something in him that would carry him through a crisis on the stage; at least he might be expected to possess a certain adaptability to the medium." Jack did possess that quality, but he was bored easily and he never learned to enjoy playing the same part night after night. "Of these early performances I have no playbills and no scrapbooks. To my mind, at least, this is just one more evidence of my attitude toward the theater," Jack explained. "I left the stage to study at art schools, and I only went back to the theater because there is hope—at least money—for the bad actor. The indifferent painter usually starves."

McKee Rankin did more than help the Barrymores get started in the theater. He and his wife Kitty Blanchard produced Lionel's first wife. In 1904 twenty-year-old Lionel wed sixteen-year-old Doris Rankin. For twenty years they would support each other personally and professionally, though they were both private people who didn't outwardly express their feelings. Michael Strange once saw Lionel kiss the collar of Doris's cape before placing it on her shoulders, a tender symbol of love that he did not expect to be observed.

Barry's resentment of Charles Frohman began with what Barry saw as management mistreating talent on tour. After Frohman made it impossible for Barry to continue touring in *Aristocracy* because the schedule would not accommodate Barry's many pets, his resentment grew into hatred. As his mind began to crumble into insanity, Barry blamed every evil on Frohman and the Theatrical Syndicate, which he vowed to fight and expose. At the turn of the twentieth century Barry was confined to an

Ethel in her early roles in *The Country Mouse* and as *Cousin Kate*.

Publicity shot of young Ethel in *Carrots* (1903).

Ethel in another of her long-touring roles, that of Miss Moffat in *The Corn Is Green*, which opened late in 1940. She toured the play almost continuously for several years.

Ethel about the time she began to work for Charles Frohman. Whenever he had a shortage of good roles for her, Ethel would tour in one of her favorite one-act plays, *The Twelve Pound Look*, which appealed in particular to her female fans.

Ethel at the age of fifty-seven, at her home in Mamaroneck, Long Island. She had just announced that she planned to retire and would devote her time to teaching promising students. Despite this announcement, she often returned to stage and screen when she found herself in need of money, and after her "retirement" she made more than twenty films.

Jack Barrymore was not Sidney Harris's first choice as a husband for his socialite daughter, but Jack, who always appealed to older women, was assisted by his future wife's grandmother, who wrote to her granddaughter, "He is so handsome. If I were a young woman, I would be crazy about him myself."

Katherine Corri Harris Barrymore, Jack's first wife. She acted with Jack in several productions, but she was disappointed with his desire to stay at home when he wasn't on the stage. Their marriage lasted seven years.

A studio portrait of handsome young Jack. When he first began his career, he often borrowed clothes for the stage (and for the street) from his uncle John Drew.

Jack in *The Fortune Hunter,* his first role to garner real appreciation for his comic talents.

Lionel with Nancy Montague in D.W. Griffith's *America* (1924).

Lionel as Captain Butler reports to George III in *America*.

asylum. He would hang on for several years, falling deeper into surly paranoia.

Maurice Herbert Barrymore, the former Herbert Blyth, died on March 25, 1905 in Amityville, New York. Barry had been in and out of a coma for days before he roused himself to say, "Our trade falls heavily upon these feeble folk"—a line from his beloved play *Najezda*. As Amy Leslie had so rightly observed, Barry was "made up of unfulfilled expectations of his friends and unfulfilled promises to himself," and now no one would ever know just how talented he had actually been and just how far he could have gone had he been interested in stardom.

Lionel could not settle down and accept his vocation as an actor. He still dreamed of painting, and he formulated a plan. He visited Ethel and asked her to stake him to a few years in Paris. He would study with the best teachers and philosophize with tomorrow's masters. He might even become a well-known artist as well. Perhaps Ethel thought of her early dreams of becoming a concert pianist, or maybe she felt self-conscious about the degree of her success. She may have just wanted Lionel to be as happy as she was. Doris and Lionel set out for Paris, where they would stay until Ethel married Russell Colt and began to raise a family. Those events told Lionel that his time had come to support himself and he returned to the place he knew he could make money—the stage.

Frohman sent Jack Barrymore on tour with Willie Collier's company in Richard Harding Davis's *The Dictator*. Collier, not a fan of Jack's casual approach to acting, had threatened to fire Jack throughout the tour, but each time Frohman talked him out of it for Ethel's sake. The tour ended, and Jack was taking in some culture in San Francisco before the company sailed for Australia. On April 17, 1906, Jack saw more than he had bargained for when the earth moved under San Francisco.

Jack enjoyed a performance of the visiting Metropolitan Opera Company of New York, went to a very late supper party, and walked home with a friend. Because of the late hour, Jack decided to stay the night, so he shed his evening clothes and tumbled into bed. Not long after, he was nearly thrown out of bed with the first great shock of the quake. He immediately put his dress clothes back on and started walking toward town. "Everywhere whole sides of houses were gone. The effect was as if someone had lined the streets with gigantic dolls' houses of the sort that have no fronts," John wrote. "People were hurriedly dressing and at the same time trying to gather and throw out what seemed most valuable to them. More prudent persons, who couldn't too readily shake off the habits of shyness nor too quickly forget their decorum, were putting up sheets to shield them from the passers-by."

As he walked, Jack saw many people he knew, and the devastation took on a surreal aspect that appealed to his sense of the bizarre. In Union Square he saw Willie Collier in "bedroom slippers and a flowered dressing gown." "Go West, young man, and blow up with the country," he called to Jack.

In front of the Palace Hotel, Jack ran into Diamond Jim Brady, who was terribly amused to see Jack in the early morning rubble in his evening dress. "When he went back East he and many others circulated this story about my dressing for an earthquake," Jack recalled. "In fact, a great deal of my reputation for eccentricity had, I think, its origin in this incident. Until I talked to Brady it had not occurred to me that I was oddly dressed for the occasion. I don't know, though, what one should wear at an earthquake."

Society and the theater crowd thrilled to Ethel Barrymore's romantic marriage to Russell Griswold Colt, son of Samuel Pomery Colt, president of the United States Rubber Company and grandson of the inventor of the Colt revolver. They were married during the Boston engagement of *Lady Frederick* in which Ethel was starring.

Ethel took no time off for a honeymoon, but continued her tour with her new husband in tow. Colt described it as a mixed up honeymoon during which the wife worked and the husband lounged, which was exactly what he would do. His father gave the couple a house in New York, and Ethel finished her tour in time to rest up for the first appearance of Samuel Pomeroy Colt, named after his paternal grandfather. Ethel began her new role as mother on November 28, 1909.

Ethel contended in the press that a woman could have a career and motherhood too. To prove her point, she stayed at home with her son for a few weeks, then she developed the method of long distance mothering that she would practice until her children were grown. In August, she and Russell left for Europe on a belated honeymoon.

Eight months after Ethel took the plunge, her younger brother Jack married Katherine Corri Harris. The press reported that Jack's bachelorhood had been insured by Lloyd's of London and that someone was making $50,000 on the union. John had been playing to standing room only crowds in *The Fortune Hunter*. He had become, like his father, a matinee idol without peer. And like his father, he had no shortage of female companionship. But in the fall of 1910 Jack saw his future bride at a coming out party. She had an immediate interest in Jack, imagining the parties and functions she would attend on the arm of America's most handsome bachelor, tamed into domesticity but no less attractive at home than on the stage.

Katherine was a beautiful girl, a debutante with little life experience. Like Lionel's bride, she was ten years younger than her intended. Artist James Montgomer Flagg was enthralled by Katherine's face and thought "she had a lovely figure…wide-shouldered, willowy."

Katherine wanted completely different things from Jack than he was willing to give her. After their wedding breakfast Jack went on to the next stop on his tour, and his wife went to stay with Ethel and Russell. Jack visited regularly, but he continued touring for a year. Then his nesting instinct began to develop. He rented a cozy apartment and furnished it by hand with rare books, silver trinkets, and furniture he sometimes antiqued with an ice pick. He had little interest in mingling with actors when he was not on stage, but preferred instead to read all night and sleep until it was time to go to the theater. He and Katherine had ferocious arguments and passionate reunions.

In 1912, a "Jack Barrymore" was credited for playing in three films—*Dream of a Motion Picture Director*, *A Prize Package*, and *The Widow Casey's Return*—but it is unclear if this actor is *the* Jack Barrymore. As Jack pointed out in *Confessions of an Actor*, he didn't keep souvenirs or records

Lionel hated playing romantic leads, and he was a brilliant character actor. He enjoyed disguising himself with eyebrows and moles, and he liked to research his parts to make his performances accurate. Here he is as Billy Bones in *Treasure Island* (1934).

about his career. Considering that acting for films had not yet become respectable in 1912, perhaps Jack was trying the new medium quietly so as not to endanger his reputation.

Lionel returned from Paris and began casting about for roles to play. The shaggy, rumpled lifestyle he had loved in Europe was gone, and he paid a visit to Billy Muldoon's health farm to shed the extra pounds he had put on.

Lionel played in eighteen films during 1912, wrote two scripts, and directed five films. The Barrymore men could be single-minded when they found something that interested them. The following year Jack probably had a part in *One on Romance*, though that sighting is unconfirmed. Lionel played in forty-two films during 1913.

When he was back in stage form, Lionel accepted an engagement to play a dragoman in Arthur Conan Doyle's *The Fires of Fate*. Some reviewers noted his new girth, but his performance was well received.

Though Jack and Lionel claimed that the Drews and the Barrymores never attempted to influence others, Ethel's shock at Lionel's next decision caused her to lash out at him in print. Lionel teamed up with Uncle Sidney Drew and his wife Gladys—on vaudeville. "If Lionel prefers Vaudeville to the legitimate theater, we can only wait till he tires of it and returns to the fold," Ethel said. Lionel ignored Ethel's criticism and began playing at Hammerstein's theater in *The Jail Bird*. When that failed, Sidney Drew produced a short play that Lionel had written. Doris played an intense part in his dark sketch about prostitution, the first role she had played with her husband.

During this period, two significant things happened to Lionel and Doris—their two-year-old daughter, Ethel, died. (Her sister, Mary, had died as an infant in Paris.) Lionel and Doris would always long for children, but Doris did not conceive again.

Wallace Beery looking over Lionel's shoulder in *Ah, Wilderness* (1935).

A postcard from Lionel's MGM days. Like Ethel, Lionel spent money quickly, so he worked up until the time his health would no longer allow it. When he was no longer able to walk, parts were written for him to play in his wheelchair.

Late in his MGM days, Lionel played the recurring role of Dr. Gillespie in the Dr. Kildare series of films. This one is *Dr. Kildare and the Glamor Girl.*

The other significant event for Lionel at this time was that McKee Rankin introduced him to D.W. Griffith, and through him Lionel discovered the screen. In 1911 he made three pictures for Griffith: *The Miser's Heart, The Battle,* and *Fighting Blood.* At this time films were made in New York and New Jersey, and Lionel felt a little squeamish about openly striding into the studio—he often went around to the back door instead of entering from the street. Griffith was not impressed with the Barrymore name or Lionel's prior experience on the stage, but he agreed to give him a try.

John and Ethel, meanwhile, co-starred in *The Slice of Life,* a comic farce in which John played a character that was a deliberate impersonation of his uncle, John Drew. In the eyes of their audiences, the two Barrymores were better than one, and the production was just the sort of

play Ethel excelled in. Ethel retired again to the Colt residence at Mamaroneck to await the arrival of Ethel Barrymore Colt, who was born May 1, 1912.

John became a star in his own right as well as the hearthrob of many a young woman in *Half a Husband.* He followed this triumph with *The Affairs of Anatole,* and *Believe Me, Xantippe.*

Ethel now began a year's vaudeville tour in Barrie's *The Twelve-Pound Look,* ending in 1913, and again returned to Mamaroneck, where John Drew Colt was born on September 9. *Tante,* a comedy, brought her back to Broadway in October.

Early the following year, after a brief appearance with her Uncle John at the Empire in *A Scrap of Paper,* she decided to investigate this new hobby of Lionel's and finally succumbed to the lure of the movies. She felt a little dirty turning to this lowly form of entertainment, but Ethel had bills to pay and, like her grandmother Mrs. John Drew, she never shirked her responsibilities.

In 1914, Ethel appeared for the first time in front of the cameras in *The Nightingale*, a screenplay especially written for her by Maurice's old friend Augustus Thomas. Her character, Isola Franti, was forced to choose between motherhood and career, an issue close to Ethel's heart. Ethel was plump after three children, and she was not particularly beautiful on film. Unlike Lionel, she put herself on a strict heath regimen and slimmed her figure of seventy-five extra pounds—without Billy Muldoon's health farm. Ethel's public cared about all details of her life. Her opinions—Yes, a woman can excell at both motherhood and career! No, a woman should never follow fashion trends!—were reported in magazines and newspapers.

The same year, Lionel made twelve films, including one of *Under the Gaslights*, the play in which his father had made his debut in Boston forty years earlier. Jack, who made two films, was becoming a popular comedian. More people had seen him in *An American Citizen* and *The Man from Mexico* than had seen him in all of his stage performances added together.

Katherine wanted to act with her husband; she was still enamored of entertainment circles. She played with Jack in Famous Players' *Nearly a King* and in Vaudeville circuits in *Anatol*. They were together on Broadway in *Believe Me, Xanthippe* and *The Princess Zim Zim*, which had been written by Jack's friend Ned Sheldon.

John had mastered light comedy and decided to turn to drama. He chose *Kick-In*, produced by Al Woods. Originally a one-act play written and performed on Vaudeville circuits by Williard Mack, the play had been expanded to feature length and beefed up with all sorts of acrobatics and escapades. The one-act play remained as the heavy scene of the play, and the rest was cops and robbers.

Sheldon was Jack Barrymore's voice of reason—Jack trusted his opinion more than he trusted his own. "No one since I have been a serious actor has been more helpful to me than Edward Sheldon," Jack wrote of his friend. "In fact I am not sure that he didn't make me a serious actor." He also made Jack a better man than he might have been on his own. He was confidant, psychiatrist, and advisor, and in a pinch he could write a part for Jack that would show his talents to advantage.

Jack was wonderful in *Kick-In*, Sheldon told him, but the vehicle was hardly a heavyweight role. Sheldon

advised his friend to find himself a completely serious role and show audiences what he could do. Jack promised to think about a role that would be without any touch of comedy. "I could paste down my moustache," he told Sheldon. But first John starred in his own real-life drama as he and Katherine divorced. "I thought it would be grand to be the wife of such a man before I married him and even later when he told me we were to part forever, I tried to win him back. His only response was that our temperaments were too different, and further living togther was impossible," she explained to the judge.

Sheldon did not let the matter of Jack playing serious drama to rest. According to Jack, "He persisted. When he found that Galsworthy's play, *Justice*, was to be put on, he arranged with the producers that I play the leading part of the defaulting clerk. I went at it with no little trepidation." The play opened in New Haven, Connecticut, where Jack had previously opened in his first comedy hit, *The Fortune Hunter*. Jack was, as Ned Sheldon had known he would be, a hit. The first night Jack had no problem escaping from prison, even though he wasn't supposed to. "When I pounded with frenzy upon my cell door in the prison, I broke right through the wood grating, which was painted black as an understudy for iron. Few persons outside the theater have any comprehension of how strong an actor is on the first night." As he usually did, Jack devalued his performance. "Though I was quite unused to serious values," he wrote, "there was in this performance in *Justice* something vital that came wholly from the desire to make good. Even though not backed up by the right technique, it had a certain gauche sincerity."

MICHAEL STRANGE was the nom de plume of Blanche Oelrichs, socialite of Newport and New York. Her mother was of minor Austrian nobility, and Blanche, at this time a beautiful woman of ambiguous gender with large dark eyes alight with creativity and desire, had grown up surrounded by wealth and aristocracy. She was a tantalizing combination of feminist and incurable romantic. Her flirtations were many, with both men and women. She had married Leonard M. Thomas, senior diplomat, at the age of eighteen. They had two sons, Leonard and Robin. Leonard Senior was much older than Blanche and though they maintained a very full social life, the boredom in their relationship made his visits to Europe on diplomatic missions a welcome relief, for Blanche at least. At the time she met Jack, Leonard was tied up with the war and would not even know he was losing his wife until she was already, technically, gone.

In her autobiography, *Who Tells Me True,* Blanche describes her first encounter with Jack Barrymore.

> I came into a smoke-filled room, where the Theater Guild Group were entertaining, and I noticed, standing in the doorway, handsome Edward Sheldon, dark haired and noble looking with such a nosily polished skin, as if he had just come in from skating. A few moments later Phil Moeller, one of the Guild's directors, asked me if he might present Mr. Barrymore, who wished to meet me. Here he was, bowing and smiling, looking very slim and nervously poetic, with grayish-green hazel eyes, of immense fascination, because they seemed to mirror back oneself in flattering, mischievous terms. He looked elfin and forsaken—an intriguing combination—but very highly strung too. His walk, slanted, oblique, seemed to say that his clothes irked his skin.

While Blanche was becoming infatuated, First Lt. Leonard Thomas was conveniently located overseas. Her family was shocked when she announced that she had fallen in love with America's greatest actor. She could not be deterred.

When Leonard Thomas returned from Europe, Blanche spoke candidly to him about her feelings for Jack Barrymore. Leonard, older and wiser, hoped that Blanche would forget about her infatuation. He exacted a promise from his wife to stay away from the object of her infatuation for six months, after which time her head would be clear and she could make a rational decision. The only problem with Leonard's plan was that Blanche had no intention of thinking with anything other than her heart.

JACK HAD ALWAYS LOVED George du Maurier's book *Peter Ibbetson.* He was such a fan that the author's son, Gerald, had given him "an original drawing by his father and a notebook which had been used during the writing of *Peter Ibbetson.* On the last page of this is the family tree of the Ibbetsons, showing the lineage of Peter, with his delightful French ancestry. It is a charming thing to possess, being so typical of the gaiety and beauty of the author's mind." Constance Collier was another big fan of the etherial romance, and she and Jack often discussed playing Ibbetson together; in early 1917 their talks became serious. There was a chance they could get Lionel

to join them. They needed a manager and a theater. Details came together when they recruited Al Woods, who had managed the production of *The Yellow Ticket,* a play that so bored Jack that he often acted up. Woods might have been a little leery of more of Jack's misbehavior, but he was savvy enough to realize that any two Barrymores in any one production meant big business. He sunk as much money into the production as he could afford.

Jack found the audience particularly receptive to the play. "It was war time, and the scenes in which the past was lived again and there were reunions with loved ones were very comforting to many persons. When we played it in Canada, where so many people had lost sons, the sympathy for the play was most unusual. The quiet, peculiar appeal hardly seemed like the theater."

After *Peter Ibbetson,* Jack decided to do an English version of Tolstoy's *The Living Corpse,* which was renamed *Redemption.* Michael Strange adapted the Russian work for the stage, though she did not receive credit for the writing. She believed that Jack should do the play, so before anyone could stop her, "she went to the sister of Joe Davidson, the sculptor, who was then running the Russian Inn in New York, and from her, she obtained a literal translation. Out of this she made an excellent adaptation, which, like most good adaptations for the theater, contained a great deal that was original."

Jack owned the rights to Sem Benelli's play, *La Cena della Belle,* and he and Ned Sheldon, who had written the English adaptation, wanted to see the two Barrymore brothers together in the production. Lionel had proven himself a versatile actor and had just made a huge hit in *The Copperhead.* Jack had bought out the house one evening to see his brother's play instead of playing *Peter Ibbetson* for Lee Schubert. Though Jack's ticket to see Lionel's performance should have cost him $3,000, Schubert declined to collect.

John underestimated the success he would have with *The Jest.* The production turned out to be "gory, passionate, colorful, and provocative." Audiences "did not seem to be able to get enough of *The Jest* and it ran and ran." The play ran for ten weeks and grossed more than $180,000.

JACK WAS NOW, without question, the biggest draw on the American stage. The word "genius" was no longer whispered about the youngest Barrymore—it began to appear in print beside Jack's name. He was at the top of his game, he had proved he was a worthy heir to his long

Jack Barrymore and second wife Blanche Oelrich, who wrote and performed under the pseudonym Michael Strange. She and Jack struck sparks off each other.

line of talented forebears, and he hadn't yet entered the most creative period of his professional life, which—not coincidentally—ran concurrently with the second of Jack's marriages—or "bus accidents" as he would call them later in life.

Leonard Thomas finally admitted defeat and released Blanche from further obligation to him. She obtained a divorce in Paris, and on August 15, 1920, she married Jack Barrymore "in a flower-bedecked room at the apartment of Mrs. John McCullogh, at the Ritz-Carlton in New York, a union of two beautiful, dramatic, temperamental people." They bought a charming little place in White Plains that was surrounded by parklike grounds. The Barrymores loved their pastoral life and alternated between New York and Europe. Jack took time off to spend with his wife, though he already had in mind his most intriguing play—yet—*Richard III*.

John took Michael to White Sulfer Springs, Virginia, to relax. Nature always soothed John. He would walk through the woods, reciting from *Richard*, giving the dark character his full concentration. He dug deep and decided that "people like this man because he is on the level of his iniquity." The play worked, Jack discovered, because "the audience is his only confidant, and that is the secret of the play's success."

Jack gave everything he had to the character of Richard. "I had to make over my voice and work unceasingly on intonations. I am afraid that when I came to the playing, I probably, with no intention of so doing, sang a great deal of the text," he wrote.

Jack's uncle, John Drew, had always said that his nephew had a lazy way of speaking that made him sound like a ruffian. Margaret Carrington, whom John later spoke of as a "white witch," agreed to work with Jack to train his voice for Shakespeare.

While Jack was recovering at Billy Muldoon's health farm after his exhausting run as Richard III, he drew this sketch of himself, expressing the duality of his psyche.

A rare shot of Jack and his elder daughter, Diana, as a baby. Though Lionel used to sneak into the nursery and cuddle the child, Jack was petrified of holding her.

Ethel as the queen in *Clair de Lune* (1921), the play Michael wrote for Jack. Even with beloved Ethel's presence in the production, the play was not a success.

To my friend John Barrymore
John S. Sargent   1923

In 1923 Jack asked John Singer Sargent to paint his portrait, but by this time Sargent was no longer painting. He agreed instead to do a sketch. Though Jack was to pay him for the pencil drawing, the artist instead insisted that the work was his holiday gift to the actor.

Carrington, sister of actor Walter Huston, had once been a singer of exceptional talent, until her vocal cords were damaged when a fish bone lodged in her throat. Because she could no longer express herself with her singing voice, she developed a method of voice improvement all her own, and she offered her training free, as a labor of love, to artists in whom she recognized potential. She jumped at the chance to train Jack's voice, and the experience was mutually satisfying. "Working with John Barrymore was like playing on a harp with a thousand strings."

Richard III was so exhausting that John suffered the first of his spells of prostration. He went to Billy Muldoon's White Plains Sanitarium, where the former wrestler forced Jack back to health with his strict regimen.

Blanche, though she was pregnant with a Barrymore heir, had by this time transformed herself entirely into Michael Strange, and fiercely loyal Jack could provide outlets for her creativity. She wrote a play for her husband based on Victor Hugo's *L'Homme Qui Rit*, which she called *Clair de Lune*. Ethel, who would do anything for her younger brother, agreed to bring her cachet to the play. She had never seen Jack so enthusiastic about work, and though she didn't care for Michael she wanted Jack to be happy. Robert Edmond Jones designed exquisite fantasy sets, and the theater world anticipated another great production. That was not to be.

And in May 1921, John became a father, and Michael was much more successful at delivering Jack's first child than she had been at *Clair de Lune*. Michael had originally planned to name her daughter Joan after her favorite saint, but on the way to the christening, she changed her mind and gave her daughter the name of the celestial huntress.

A child could not, however, cement the two tempestuous egos into a solid relationship. They fought violently, reducing furniture to firewood on several continents. Many years later Diana Barrymore would describe her parents: "They were in competition with each other as artists, as lovers, as parents; each insisted on being the only focus… each had an uncontrollable temper." These were hardly the qualities necessary for making a happy home life. Jack continued to long for a real home, where he could put on his slippers and smoking jacket and read and drink in peace. He needed the right partner to make that vision real.

While Michael worked on *Clair*, John did a film for First National called *The Lotus Eater* (1921). The film was a light and airy interlude in which Jack's character escaped from civilization in a balloon. Jack, a sea lover, was the only

player who didn't become seasick when a boat took the cast and crew off the coast of Florida. Colleen Moore was taken with Jack's tanned, fit body and his sea-worthiness. Every evening after work he would climb the mast, stand there in the sun with his bronzed skin glistening, then plunge like a bullet into the sea below.

Alexander Woollcott, found Michael Strange's *Clair de Lune* lacking; he described it as "feeble much of the time and incorrigibly pretentious." The characters spoke lines such as, "She is like a succession of masks seen at dawn." The audience was filled with Blanche's society friends and Jack's acting chums.

The characters of *Clair de Lune* were vaguely familiar to readers of Victor Hugo—the mountebank who was terribly disfigured and the blind girl who falls in love with him. Ethel played the Queen. The dialogue was strange, and try as she might, Ethel was unable to interpret it in her usual style. The play did run for more than sixty performances, perhaps as a curiosity.

When Jack read the initial reviews of *Clair*, he announced to Ethel that he was going to speak to the second-night audience before the curtain rose and disparage the critics who had panned his wife's efforts. Ethel summoned Uncle John Drew to talk some sense into John, but his advice was disregarded. Next, Lionel appeared and threatened to strangle Jack, which impressed upon him the simple fact that the Barrymores and the Drews did not lower themselves to respond to criticism. Jack contented himself with writing a scathing letter to the *Times*, with a copy to the *Tribune*, accusing several prominent critics of not being able to think and write at the same time. The letter was never published.

"Then came *Hamlet*," Jack wrote in an understatement of the first magnitude. Jack had not read Hamlet in its entirety until he decided to play it. "I was amazed to find how simple *Hamlet* seemed to be, and I was no little bewildered that anything of such infinite beauty and simplicity should have acquired centuries of comment," Jack wrote. All the comment that is necessary upon *Hamlet* Goethe wrote in *Wilhelm Miester*: 'To me it is clear that Shakespeare sought to depict a great deed laid upon a soul unequal to the performance of it.' Jack would also perceive an incestuous angle between Hamlet and Gertrude that would shock and tantalize audiences.

Once again, Robert Edmond Jones designed magnificent sets for the play, and Arthur Hopkins eagerly produced it. Jack again went to Margaret Carrington for help, and she took him once again under her wing. She told

Hopkins the only way she would take on the work necessary to transform Jack into Hamlet was if the producer promised not to set a date for the opening until she notified him that Jack was ready. Hopkins promised.

Carrington and Barrymore sequestered themselves at her estate in Connecticut and began to work on something that would deeply offend George Bernard Shaw but would delight many theatergoers by producing a new vision of Hamlet—they began to cut the words of the bard.

After the incredibly successful run of *Hamlet* in New York, John had, by his natural talent and his determination to prove himself, produced what some believed to be the greatest Hamlet of all time. He was compared to all the other stars who had ever played the role, and the debate would rage for years. For Ethel, seeing Jack's triumph—a height that none of the other Barrymores would ever reach—was "the fulfillment of all I had ever hoped for him and more."

When Jack decided to take his Hamlet across the Atlantic to Shakespeare's homeland, Arthur Hopkins refused to produce it, fearing that Jack would be assassinated, as some British wit had suggested, or at least laughed off the stage. Hopkins did loan Jack the costumes and Jones's sets.

Jack suffered disappointment as he tried to find a venue for the production, which he was undertaking on his own, producing and directing. "This added responsibility was a delight, as there was such a splendid sense of collaboration and helpfulness everywhere. The company was interested extraordinarily by the way it was staged; this was quite new for Shakespeare in London," Jack recalled proudly. He sunk $25,000 of his own money into the production, and he finally arranged to play at the Haymarket Theatre. He was delighted to be playing where his father had played before him. (In fact, according to family lore, the Haymarket had been the place that Barry saw the playbill from which he lifted the Barrymore surname.) "The rehearsals of Hamlet were more fun than anything I have ever done," Jack raved.

On opening night, Jack was not sure what to expect on the other side of the curtain. "The effect of this upon a fairly nervous American in London, who is about to appear in the best play that London has produced, can well be imagined," he observed. Jack claimed that the business manager of the theater repeatedly came to the door of his dressing room to announce the arrival of prominent audience members. Before the time for Jack to appear on stage, he had heard that the audience included Shaw, Masefield, "Dunsany, Maugham, Mary Anderson, the Asquiths, Sir Anthony Hope Hawkins, Henry Arthur Jones, Pontius Pilate, Paul of Tarses, and the Pope." Jack described his state of mind as "the same sense of detachment I imagine that one would feel on the way to the guillotine."

He needn't have worried about his reception. After all, people pointed out, his father *was* British. While talk of Jack's Hamlet as the best ever was less in evidence than it had been in America, no one said that Jack turned in anything but inspired performances for the nine week run. "The last night I look back to as the pleasantest I have ever spent in the theater. There was enthusiasm all through the play, and at the end, when I stood with the company to acknowledge the applause, there were cries of 'Come back,'" Jack wrote later. He gave a party for the cast and crew on stage after the final performance. Ever democratic, he invited "the entire company, the stage hands, the carpenters, the electricians and everyone connected with the Haymarket Theater in any capacity whatsoever. The charwoman and cleaners sat upon the steps of Elsinore and drank Cointreau."

Among John Barrymore's remaining possessions is a copy of "The World's Greatest Tragedy," a study of *Hamlet* sent to him in 1924 by Robert M. LaFollette, a Shakespeare scholar and U.S. Senator from Wisconsin. Jack seems to have studied it closely; he underlined a number of passages that illuminated Hamlet's character as Shakespeare's "highest conception of man." Though John had already played Hamlet in the U.S. by the time he received LaFollette's analysis, he must have felt a shimmer of recognition when he read and underlined the passage that reads: "Can anyone fail to see that, from his relation to his whole environment, his attitude to everything and to everyone about him is changed?"

Jack Barrymore was changed by *Hamlet*. He had reached the pinnacle of his power, and he had fulfilled his destiny. He would never again feel obligated to apologize for work he had or had not done—he had a wonderful power.

Portrait of Michael Strange from the frontispiece of her autobiography, *Who Tells Me True,* published in 1940.

Jack and Blanche sometimes expressed their solidarity by dressing alike. Ethel said the fashions Blanche designed embarrassed Jack, but he left no comment on them. Jack and Blanche found that their creative and volatile natures brought out the worst in each other as well as some shining moments.

Jack as François Villon in *The Beloved Rogue* (1927).

Lobby card for *Rasputin and the Empress* (1932), the only film in which all three of the Great Barrymores starred.

Jack's interpretation of Mr. Hyde (1920). He loved playing character roles that allowed him to disguise his handsome face.

Jack as Beau Brummel, with Mary Astor, who was his favorite leading lady until the day he caught sight of Dolores Costello.

Jack as Dr. Jekyll, Mr. Hyde's alter ego, with Nita Naldi.

Jack has been called the greatest Hamlet of his time. His interpretation was daring: He suggested an incestuous relationship between his character and his mother Gertrude. Here Jack is playing opposite Blanche Yurka, circa 1921.

The Royal Couple

AFTER HIS LONDON run of Hamlet, Jack Barrymore came back to America a changed man. Those who saw him debark could not help but notice it. He swaggered off the ship with a small monkey on his shoulder and a British valet who was used to working for actors following behind him. But the real change was that Jack had vowed that he would never set foot on the stage again, and he would keep that promise until very near the end of his life. Jack didn't even bother to settle again in New York. Those days were over. He went straight to Hollywood.

Jack Barrymore was just what the Warner brothers had been looking for—a talented big name to make people take them seriously. At the time, the biggest star they had was Rin Tin Tin. Jack Barrymore's stock was as high as it had ever been. Not only did they offer him a huge salary for the time, they agreed to spring for accommodations at the Ambassador Hotel for Jack, Clementine the monkey, and the British valet. He would have his choice of films and leading ladies.

So now the Great Profile was lounging around the Warner Brothers lot waiting for filming to begin on his new production of *The Sea Beast*. The scenario did not strictly follow Melville, and the cynical and well-read Barrymore found that amusing. Ahab now had an evil brother and a virginal love interest who had replaced the white whale in Ahab's passions.

Barrymore stood smoking on a studio balcony, out of sorts because his current leading lady, Mary Astor, was unavailable to star with him. He was being forced to make do with pretty little Priscilla Bonner. He looked down and noticed several women, one tall and substantial and two slim, golden fawns with fair skin and large, smoky eyes.

They were kind, too. The three had stopped to give coins to a war veteran who was begging near the studio gate.

The one who had her purse open stopped as though she could feel Jack's stare upon the halo of her yellow hair. She glanced up. Their eyes did not quite meet; instead hers swept away and back to her mother and sister. Jack thought about dashing for brush and canvas to record "the most preposterously lovely creature" he had ever seen while her perfect form was still vivid in his mind. He knew, however, that he would not be able to portray a likeness that was even close to the reality of her beauty. But for a moment he felt young and full of promise.

It must have been fate. That evening he saw her face again, this time in the projection room. She had been a Wampas Baby Star in 1926 along with Joan Crawford, Mary Astor, Janet Gaynor, and Dolores Del Rio, he was told, and she had just been signed by Warner Bros. as one of their ingenues. "Get her here tomorrow morning," Jack said. Nineteen-year-old Dolores Costello was immediately notified that Mr. Barrymore would require her presence on the set the following morning.

Barrymore arranged for shooting to begin with the climax of the big love scene. He reassured the nervous beauty and gazed down into her eyes before he took her in his arms under the branches of a flowering tree. "If you are frightened," he said, "just tell me and we'll stop." He pulled her toward him and looked into her smokey eyes before he covered her trembling lips with his. The kiss was long and passionate. The scene was perfect the first time. "Cut!" the director called. "Cut!" But Barrymore took his time finishing the kiss. When he released his new leading lady, she lay in his arms in a dead faint.

Another piece of the legend that was Barrymore.

Souvenir program for *The Sea Beast* (1926), the first film in which Jack and future wife Dolores Costello starred together. At the time Jack was the biggest thing that Warner Brothers had going for them. They billed him as "The World's Foremost Actor" and reminded audiences of the great characters he had played, such as Beau Brummel, Dr. Jekyll, Hamlet, and Jacques Leroi in *The Lotus Eater* (1921). And now, Ahab—"Never was there such a role and never such an actor to play it!" Nineteen-year-old Dolores had been a performer all her life, but even she hadn't expected to go from new Warners' ingenue to leading lady playing opposite the studio's biggest star in one day. The souvenir was so thorough that it also introduced the director and writers, and commended the "trained battalions" that were working behind the scenes. For trivia buffs, a sidebar contained statistics about the great Sea Beast itself.

Characters in the Cast

"DEREK"

"REV. JOHN HARPER"

"FEDALLAH"

Dolores Costello as "Esther"

"PERTH"

"FLASH"

"QUEEQUEG"

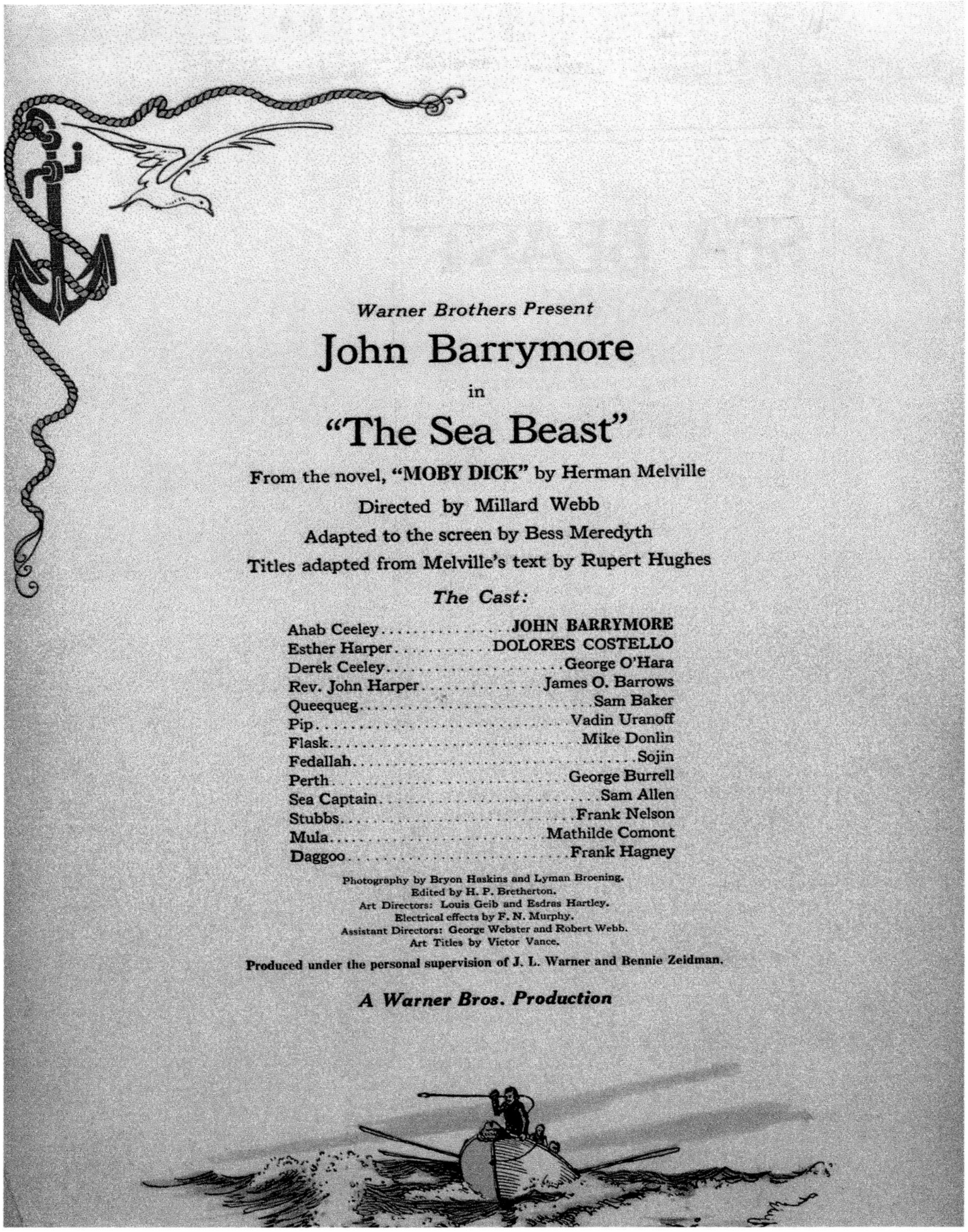

Warner Brothers Present

John Barrymore

in

"The Sea Beast"

From the novel, **"MOBY DICK"** by Herman Melville

Directed by Millard Webb

Adapted to the screen by Bess Meredyth

Titles adapted from Melville's text by Rupert Hughes

The Cast:

Ahab Ceeley	**JOHN BARRYMORE**
Esther Harper	DOLORES COSTELLO
Derek Ceeley	George O'Hara
Rev. John Harper	James O. Barrows
Queequeg	Sam Baker
Pip	Vadin Uranoff
Flask	Mike Donlin
Fedallah	Sojin
Perth	George Burrell
Sea Captain	Sam Allen
Stubbs	Frank Nelson
Mula	Mathilde Comont
Daggoo	Frank Hagney

Photography by Bryon Haskins and Lyman Broening.
Edited by H. P. Bretherton.
Art Directors: Louis Geib and Esdras Hartley.
Electrical effects by F. N. Murphy.
Assistant Directors: George Webster and Robert Webb.
Art Titles by Victor Vance.

Produced under the personal supervision of J. L. Warner and Bennie Zeidman.

A Warner Bros. Production

"The SEA BEAST"

AN EPIC

THE whaling days are gone. No longer do four-masters sail forth from New Bedford to scour uncharted seas for the Leviathan of the deep. The breed of salt water men who feared neither the gales which swept the sky nor the monsters beneath the sea, has passed.

"The Sea Beast" preserves for future generations the romance of those days of 1840. In this hour you live the lives of those sturdy adventurers, you suffer their wounds, ache in your heart for their lost loves and glory with them in their triumphant battle with the sperm whale.

There is no group of men, no business so enthralling and no period whose annals are so inspiring as those of the days when men hunted the mammoths of the sea.

The whaling days are deserving of this memorable poem—"The Sea Beast"—an epic written in the twentieth century's greatest medium—*the motion picture*.

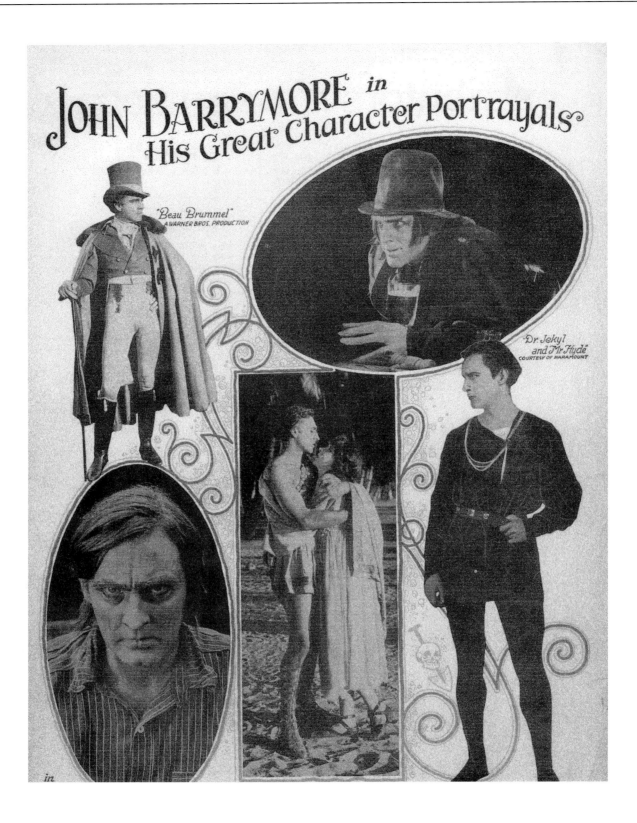

JOHN BARRYMORE
The World's Foremost Actor

JOHN BARRYMORE is more than a name; more than a personality; he is a world institution. He is more widely known among theatre-goers in all civilized countries than any other actor of the century. He achieved his world wide pre-eminence through his startling characterizations in motion pictures and today he stands as the world's greatest actor.

America has long known the adaptable versatility which marks his genius on both stage and screen. It remained for such an outstanding picture success as the Warner classic "Beau Brummel," to bring him before the vast theatre-going public of the world. Last year he added to his stage laurels by his appearance in London as "Hamlet" and all Europe applauded.

Other great actors of the stage have essayed motion pictures but the two mediums are far apart; only native genius may successfully leap from the foot-lights to the silent screen. This John Barrymore has done. Today his screen impersonations are more widely known and discussed than any other stage or screen successes. Where stage audiences are limited to thousands, millions see picture portrayals.

His interpretation of Captain Ahab in "The Sea Beast" lifts John Barrymore above every previous effort on the screen. In this role are those contrasting values which make for truly great acting. The shy, tender love of youth fires to passion beneath the soft moonlight of tropic nights; a gay heart with every promise of fulfilled happiness sails away; a sturdy man gives battle to the monster of the deep and is torn and crippled for life. Fear of pity ages this youth and when Fate mocks him into the belief that the girl he loves has been won by another, hate scorches his soul and desire for vengeance writes its hideous lines upon the face once lighted by love. Transition upon transition: youth and love and honest ambition; the terror of a soul struggling against the madness of revenge unsatisfied; and the escape of Ahab from his self made horror. Never was there such a role and never such an actor to play it!

The pedestal of Barrymore's popularity mounts higher with every production. John Barrymore is a world institution.

Contributors to the Magnificence
of "The Sea Beast"

Millard Webb

FROM extra on the lot to director of the foremost actor of the world in ten years! That is the surprising leap to fame accomplished by Millard Webb, director of "The Sea Beast." Born and bred in Kentucky in 1893, Webb began his career as a civil engineer. He was seriously injured in 1915 and went to Los Angeles to recuperate. Motion pictures appealed to his imagination and he became an extra under D. W. Griffith. Warner Bros. recognized Webb's ability and engaged him to adapt and co-direct "Brass." Collaborations on "Tiger Rose," "The Golden Cocoon" and "The Dark Swan" were followed by writing "The Marriage Vow" and "My Wife and I." He directed these last four pictures and was then selected to produce "The Sea Beast" with America's greatest actor in the star role.

Bess Meredyth

THE adaptation of Herman Melville's brilliant literary classic, "Moby Dick," was entrusted to Bess Meredyth. It was from her continuity that "The Sea Beast" was directed. There is no woman writing for the screen today who has contributed so much to genuine screen values as Bess Meredyth. Her good counsel and experience were summoned to Rome for the completion of "Ben Hur." Among her noted pictures are "Strangers of the Night," "The Famous Mrs. Fair," "The Dangerous Age" and "One Clear Call." Miss Meredyth wrote continuities for several prominent productions before the arrival of John Barrymore to make "The Sea Beast." Upon the completion of that she was assigned to "Don Juan," and is now working on the continuity of "The Tavern Knight" by Rafael Sabatini, which will be another Barrymore starring vehicle.

Rupert Hughes

NO modern writer has so completely responded to the demands of the screen as Rupert Hughes, whose novels are read by millions. In two decades Rupert Hughes has become one of the outstanding names in American literature. In addition, this remarkable man has written original scenarios and has directed his own stories. He knows to the minutest detail those intangible qualities known as "screen values." One of the most difficult tasks connected with a great picture is titling it. The writer of subtitles must be skilled in film editing. He must know what to write, and where to insert the title. Rupert Hughes was engaged to write the finished titles because in this art Hughes is a master. He stands supreme and his best work is in "The Sea Beast."

AN ARMY OF WORKERS BEHIND THE SCENES

TO make a super-production like "The Sea Beast" requires an army of men and women—an army comprising three trained battalions.

First, one division must spend months in research—to learn exactly what is required in preparation. No "props" can be made, no locations selected until it has finished its task.

Follow then the ship-builders, the town-makers, the costumers—the vast force of creators of atmosphere and constructors of environment, needed for the proper garbing of both characters and scenes.

Consider after these the diversified personnel in the picture itself: The crew of the ship, some of them appearing to justify the description, "scum," hurled at them by their not too considerate skipper. The crowds of hangers-on on the docks—representative townpeople and wharf rats mingling together. The hundreds of villagers—street crowds, the socially-elect at the reception and the grim-visaged habitues of the waterfront dives.

No wonder that for months the entire facilities of Warner Bros. West Coast Studios—Jack L. Warner, production chief, and Bennie Zeidman, his associate executive, in charge—had to be given over to "The Sea Beast." No wonder the employment of a legion of experts and of extras was made necessary.

"Give me a rip-snorting story, one that's full of action and life," John Barrymore demanded when subjects for his latest picture were under discussion, and "Moby Dick" was chosen. As alluring as the old tales of the western frontier, are the stories of the whalers. Today the whaling vessel is as much of a memory as the prairie schooner is, and this meant a vast amount of research work.

"The Sea Beast" isn't a studio lot picture. The storm scenes were not made to order in a "tank." The mountainous waves that break over "The Pequod" of New Bedford, from stem to stern, are real waves; the torrential rain is real rain, and the furious blasts that drive it horizontally into the leathern faces of the crew of real sailors are blasts of a terrific storm wind actually encountered at sea.

Ninety-eight men, and everything in the way of "props" that might conceivably be needed, were crowded upon an old whaling ship, which was towed out to sea in the teeth of a furious gale one morning before dawn. It was a strange adventure, and a terrible one. Under gigantic seas the ship quivered and creaked and groaned.

The adventure, which more than once came perilously near

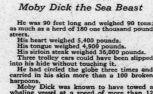

Moby Dick the Sea Beast

He was 90 feet long and weighed 90 tons; as much as a herd of 180 one thousand pound steers.

His heart weighed 5,400 pounds.
His tongue weighed 4,900 pounds.
His sirloin steak weighed 36,000 pounds.
Three trolley cars could have been slipped into his hide without touching it.
He had circled the globe three times and carried in his skin more than a 100 broken harpoons.

Moby Dick was known to have towed a whaling vessel at a speed of more than 12 knots against the wind with all sails set.

This was the creature against which Ahab (John Barrymore) pitted his puny strength and conquered, only to be conquered himself in turn by a slip of a girl (Dolores Costello) back in the sleepy old town of New Bedford.

developing into a tragedy for more than one of the ninety-eight, continued for eighteen days. When the vessel put into Los Angeles harbor again, both the craft and its human cargo were battered and bruised and worn. Probably no greater hardships ever had been endured in the making of a picture. These men had struggled through the greatest storm that land or sea ever committed to the screen. And John Barrymore had been in his element as the master of this hell ship, experiencing the hardest, most strenuous, work of his notable career.

There was romance in the selection of a man to direct this mighty picture. Millard Webb is one of the very youngest directorial geniuses in the movie world. Jack L. Warner, quick to recognize talent in a director as well as in an actor, decided upon Webb and the completed "Sea Beast" fully justifies his judgment. Bess Meredyth, who wrote the scenario, worked on location and in the studio just as strenuously as did the men.

Radio played its part in the production. Twelve loud-speakers, distributed over an area of seven acres, were used to transmit the commands of the director to two thousand "extras" on the Javanese village set. The commands of the director were thus transmitted all over the immense outdoor set at the same instant even though the players themselves could not see the director, nor he see his people.

But there were heart-aches, too. More than 600,000 feet of film was exposed in photographing "The Sea Beast." Ninety-eight per cent of this enormous footage had to be discarded. It was inevitable that there should not in every instance be entire agreement among star, director and scenarist as to just what best could be spared. Men and women who create are often unable to see all values in the same light. But again the spirit of co-operation in the Warner Studios proved supreme to individual wishes, and the fine continuity of action is the result.

Commanding such an enormous field exercises the wisdom and executive ability of an army general. Not only must the radio directions be clear and distinct but there must be lieutenants in every sector, ready to take the extras "over the top" and into the scene. These movements of bodies of men and women are timed to the second. There must be no delay; crowds must assemble at certain points at exact time and in the exposing of negative this becomes a question of seconds and not minutes. Millard Webb's arrangements for the handling of these scenes proved him to be gifted with those traits which make for a real army officer.

I hung my sister Sally,
And swung her in the galley,
So hang, boys! HANG!

The whaling ship used in the filming of *The Sea Beast.*

Jack Barrymore and Dolores Costello, in their roles as Ahab and Esther, say goodbye before Ahab departs.

A crowded dockside scene.

Esther and Ahab share a passionate embrace in the Harper house garden, the famous scene in which Dolores fainted in John's arms.

Jack and Clementine the monkey on the mast of the whaler.

Ahab and his crew
members in a lull
before the storm.

Ahab ready with
harpoon.

The harpooned
Moby Dick
pulling the skiff,
followed closely
by the whaler.

Performing his
own stunt, Jack
falls overboard
after harpooning
the whale.

After landing in the water, Ahab becomes entangled in the lines holding the whale.

Ahab loses his leg to Moby Dick.

A crewmate and fellow amputee shows Ahab how to use a wooden leg.

Brother Derek consoling Ahab.

An emotional scene as Esther sits weeping on the floor beneath the crippled Ahab.

Ahab peering through Esther's doorway into a party.

A confrontation between Derek (George O'Hara) and Ahab on the porch of the Harper house.

Ahab standing on the prow of his ship just before the madness sets in.

Jack was proud of his twisted visage as the demented whaler Ahab.

Alone in his cabin, Ahab fashions a harpoon.

Ahab in his cabin speaking to a member of his crew.

Captain Ahab recruiting new crew members in a tavern.

A crazed Ahab
in a whaling
skiff chases
Moby Dick.

Ahab and Queequeg
on the deck.

Captain Ahab
contemplating
whether or not to
take the hand
offered to him.

Jack and Dolores in their roles as Chevalier Fabien des Grieux and Manon Lascaut on the set of *When a Man Loves* (1927).

Cartoon by James Montgomery Flagg lampooning Jack and Dolores's film *When a Man Loves*.

Des Grieux and Manon in a tender moment.

Des Grieux in a tavern with the barkeep.

Des Grieux and Manon in bed.

Conte de Morfontaine confronting des Grieux.

Barrymore with Clementine the monkey, a gift from actress Gladys Cooper. Clementine acted in a number of Jack's films.

Though later Clementine developed a violent jealousy of Dolores, here she sits on the actress's lap.

Irene Fenwick Barrymore, Lionel, Dolores, and Jack in costume, and Allan Crosland, director, on the set of *When a Man Loves.*

Des Grieux and Manon with the monkey.

Dolores helps publicize *Noah's Ark* (1929), in which she played two characters, Miriam in Biblical times (above and top right) and Mary in modern times.

In the doodles he made
while he was with Dolores,
Jack often pictured himself as
a dark cat. Here he is watching
Dolores's new movie.

Darryl Zanuck, Jack Warner, Dolores Costello, Albert Warner, and William Koenig pose at the Warner Brothers lot during the making of *Noah's Ark*.

While Dolores was busy with *Noah's Ark*, Jack was unhappy on the set of *Eternal Love* (1929). The film, directed by Ernst Lubitsch, was filmed in Lake Louise, Canada, where Jack was forced to spend six weeks away from Dolores. German actress Camilla Horn starred with him in what would be Lubitsch's final silent film.

John Decker, Jack's friend, sketched this depiction of brooding Jack with Camilla Horn from *Eternal Love*.

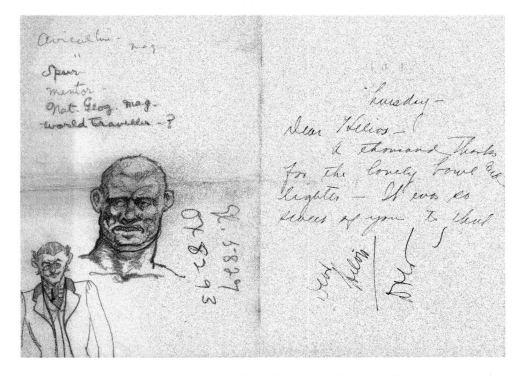

Dolores began a thank you note to Helios Hotchener, the wife of Jack's business manager, and when she discarded it Jack enhanced it with his sketches.

The Goddess of the Silent Screen and the Great Profile—Dolores and Jack Barrymore—at the beginning of their marriage.

The Mariner, the yacht Jack and Dolores used during their early travels, would carry the couple on their extensive honeymoon. When John was young he dreamed of repeating Darwin's voyages on *The Beagle*, and at the height of his career he had the money and means to visit some places the naturalist had described.

Here Dolores holds a curlew she killed on her first shot. Though she had never hunted before she met Jack, she was a good sport.

Jack and Dolores following in Darwin's footsteps on the beach of one of the Galapagos Islands.

Jack enjoys a natural waterfall.

Jack and Dolores aboard the *Mariner* with a huge manta ray they harpooned off Cocos Island, Costa Rica.

Dolores and Jack with a shark they bagged.

Jack and Dolores watch a group of iguanas in the Galapagos Islands. Jack inherited his father's affection for unusual animals.

Dolores explores the beach.

Dolores pets a more familiar animal at the Carlos Gils island ranch.

Jack and Dolores pose with their Ecuadorian hosts. On the wall of the dwelling, they found a wrinkled clipping about their wedding.

Jack holds a young seal next to his catch of caravelle.

Dolores's turn to pose with the fish.

The couple discovers
a giant heron's nest.

Dolores explores on horseback, guided by Señor Alvarez.

Jack and Dolores on the steps of a church in Quito, surrounded by native Ecuadorians.

A man operating a bicycle pontoon in Guayaquil harbor, Ecuador.

The square in front of the Hotel Berlin in Huigia before the unveiling of the statue of Eloy Alfaro.

Dolores with Sister Mary in front of the convent of the Immaculate Conception in Huigia.

Jack sits for a haircut on the deck of *The Mariner*.

Jack's sketches of Ecuadorian natives.

As their trip draws to a close, Jack and Dolores pose on the Biana River in Balboa, Panama, with the alligators they captured.

For my own winklis ...
on their first anniversary.

Hoonick —

On their first anniversary Jack depicts himself, Dolores, and baby Dede as a cozy cat family.

Shortly after the honeymoon, Jack purchased this 120-foot diesel yacht. Movietone News filmed as Jack made a brief speech and Dolores christened the ship *The Infanta*.

Little Dede on the deck of *The Infanta*.

Dolores shows off her fishing pole and a blue marlin.

To:
Dolores · Ethel · Mae ·
on her christening ·
from her father ·

Jack commonly depicted himself as a
bum in the diary he kept on his honeymoon and dedicated to Mae Costello.
The letter at left was written for Dede
on her christening day and the one
below commemorated her first hair cut.

My own Darling HooniKinder·

She has been such a
dear good egg – and he loves
it so much –!
Dingbat –

A family portrait.

Dede and her nurse next to a large sea bass.

Captain Otto Mathias
and crew find whale
vertebrae on an island
in Mexican waters.

Dolores, Dede, and Jack
Barrymore on *The Infanta*.

Dolores, Dede, and Jack on the studio lot while Jack was making *The Mad Genius* (1931).

Jack and Dolores with host Joe Ibach and his wife, Muz, in front of their Alaskan cabin.

In Alaska, Jack bought a tribal totem pole, which the crewmen helped him remove and haul back to California. Lionel said Jack's bad luck started when he erected it on his property on Tower Road.

Jack desperately wanted a son. In Alaska he heard the superstition that a woman who eats the heart of a bear will give birth to a male child.

Dolores consented to try the bear's heart. In June of 1932, she would give birth to John Barrymore Jr.

Dolores and Jack with newborn John Jr. He already has his thick black hair and intense eyes.

Dolores holds Dede and Helene Costello holds John Jr. at his christening. Jack and Lionel, standing in for godfather Ned Sheldon, are behind.

Seated: Irene, Lionel, Ethel, Dolores, Dede, Jack, and John Jr. Standing: Jackie Colt, Ethel Colt, and Sammy Colt, gathered in the library of the Bel Air Hotel during the making of *Rasputin and the Empress*.

Introducing John Barrymore Jr. in the garden of the Bel Air Hotel.

The Great Barrymores
and the youngest, who
seems impressed.

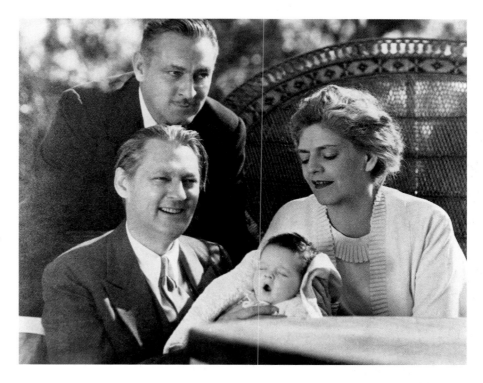

Dolores and her children relaxing on the deck of *The Infanta*.

Dede, Dolores, and John Jr.
John took his first steps on deck.

Dede dressed as
a sailor on dock
in Alaska.

Jack and John Jr. in a tender moment.

Jack designed a family crest he called a "snake regnant." Here the snake wearing a crown is shown on a flag Jack had made for *The Infanta*.

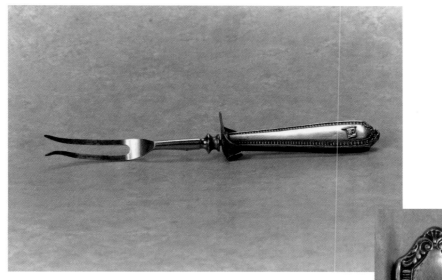

The snake regnant also adorns the Barrymore silverware.

Artist Willy Pogany and Jack Barrymore admire Pogany's painting of Jack and his family in 1933.

Opposite: John Jr. and the remains of the bear.

N MANY WAYS, Jack Barrymore *was* the history of film. He was in the audience the first time Hollywood heard synchro-nized sound on film, and he was there on the screen as well.

Sam Warner and his brothers chose *Don Juan* as the first feature-length film their studio would release with synchronized sound. It had already been shown from August 1926 until October without sound, to give engineers enough time to install Vitagraph speakers and equipment in Warner theaters. The production was "lav-ish, exuberant fun," and audiences had no complaints about it as a silent. The Warners thought it was an ideal film for their first sound experiment—not so heavy that it would render the music ineffective, and not so light that the music would overwhelm it. Fortunately for their studio and for all of America, they were right.

In October a distinguished crowd gathered at Grauman's Egyptian Theatre, the only theater on the West Coast that was set up for Vitaphone, to hear what sound was all about. When the show began at 8:30, nearly 1,800 people had taken their seats— John Barrymore, Mary Astor, Charlie Chaplin, and Cecil B. DeMille among them. First to appear on the screen was the elfin Will Hays, who congratulated Bell Laborato-ries, Western Electric, and American Telegraph and Telephone, who had jointly developed the Vitaphone technology. In the "first speech ever recorded for talking pictures,"

Hays clearly had a sense of himself in an historic moment, but in the end it didn't matter what he said. The audience was so enthralled with the concept of synchroniza-tion that gasps filled the air as Hays's voice echoed and reverberated. When he finished speaking, the delighted crowd went wild.

Following Hays were several musical shorts, including a song by Giovanni Martinelli and a serenade by the New York Philharmonic Orchestra. The audience was moved by the voice of Martinelli, and they were stunned by the footage of the Philharmonic, in which the film cut from one instrument to another, the sound fol-lowing in perfect sync.

Don Juan was a swashbuckler of epic pro-portions. Pale women exuded sexual ten-sion. Characters were tortured, put out of commission in sword fights, and walled up in old houses. The sound of swords clanging, doors slamming, and bells ringing was per-fectly timed. As always, Barrymore was mag-nificent in tights, dueling with weapons and dallying in boudoirs, though he always said he hated playing "sweet-scented jackass" roles. He bestowed 191 kisses during the ninety-minute film: a little over two per minute. At one point John Barrymore leapt from his seat, clambered over the knees of his compatriots, and ran into Sid Grauman's office. Once there, he was reportedly speech-less. When the film ended, the audience jumped to its feet as one and was deafened by its own applause and "boot thunder."

Jack in *General Crack* (1930).

Dolores and her children relaxing on the deck of *The Infanta*.

The Great Barrymores
and the youngest, who
seems impressed.

Introducing John Barrymore Jr. in the garden of the Bel Air Hotel.

Jack the hypnotist and Marian Marsh as Trilby in *Svengali* (1931). Though the title character now seems unattractive, at the time of the film's release, women found his sad manipulations and his unrequited longing appealing.

Publicity for *Svengali*.

A lobby card advertising MGM's all-star production of *Grand Hotel* (1932), starring Jack as Baron Felix von Geigern and Greta Garbo as the washed-up ballet dancer he romances.

Lionel Barrymore as Kringelein the humble clerk who finds happiness, Joan Crawford as the stenographer Flaemmchen, and Jack as Baron von Geigern in *Grand Hotel*.

Vincent Sherman, who would later direct Lionel and Drew Barrymore, stars with Jack in *Counsellor at Law* (1933). Photo from Sherman's collection.

Jack in *Twentieth Century* (1934).

Jack in a somber pose.

The Costellos

I have such memories as few men can boast. People have loved me. That's enough of an epitaph for me.

—MAURICE COSTELLO

MAURICE GEORGE COSTELLO was born February 22, 1877, in Pittsburgh, Pennsylvania, to Thomas Costello and Ellen Fitzgerald Costello, both from County Kerry, Ireland. The name Costello is Spanish, "both Histrionic and Apostolic," according to Maurice's cousin Brother Brendan. "St. James the Apostle spent his life and died in Spain. And was interred in the little town of Compostello from whom it took its name, corrupted from Corpus Apostoles to Compostello, then there retaining, you have your name— it gives its name to one of the Baronies of Ireland." The Costellos themselves carried the blood of Spaniards and Irishmen, just as their name symbolized. Their family crest was a falcon bearing an olive branch, their motto "Audax fortuna jovat" (fortune favors the brave), according to Brendan.

Maurice and his two sisters grew up in the neighborhood of 43rd or 45th Streets near Butler. When he was five or six, he was enrolled at the Old Forbes School between Magee and Stevenson Streets in the old Sixth Ward. Even then he enjoyed performing for his classmates, although he was a good student as well.

Thomas Costello died while working at the Carnegie Steel Mill in Pittsburgh when his children were young. After his death, Ellen Fitzgerald Costello married William

Vincent Paul Coiness, a Lithuanian who had been in this country a number of years and was enormously proud of his American citizenship. He was employed by the Schenly Park Conservatory.

In June 1900 Maurice left Pittsburgh for New York City. The twenty-two year old spent the rest of the year touring around the South and Midwest in a variety of stage plays. This same year Maurice learned of a cousin, also named Maurice Costello (and both of them named for their grandfather), who was living in Emmetsburg, Iowa. Maurice G. wrote to Maurice J., and on December 4th he received his answer. "So you are Thomas Costello's son," wrote the Maurice from Iowa. "Well then you and I are first cousins. Your father and my father were brothers by the same father. But your father's mother was the second wife of Maurice Costello, our grandfather. Your grandmother was a Harnahan; my grandmother was a Murphy. I think your father's mother is still alive. She was married a second time to Timothy Carroll." Typical of the very religious Roman Catholic family, he ended the letter with, "Be sure to go to mass every Sunday. Are you with a clean company?"

The Costello family worried greatly about Maurice's choice of careers. He was the only member of his immediate family to leave Pittsburgh, and then, to leave it for the

Early in his career with
Vitagraph, Maurice Costello
was known only as "Dimples."
He received bags of fan mail
asking, "What is your name?"

stage! Nearly all of his relatives had chosen to serve the
Church, and at the turn of the twentieth century the
whole Costello family was praying for Maurice to come to
his senses and return to the city of his birth. Brother
Brendan wrote to him on June 24th, 1901, from
Presentation Monastery, Mount St. Joseph, Cork, Ireland.
"How long did you stay with your family?" he inquired.
"How glad I'd feel to see you at home there again. That
dangerous calling you are at, afrights me. You cannot see
it as it is nor its dangers which are many and frightful.
Give my best regards to your mother. She is anxious about
you, too. All who see your dangers could not be otherwise. Do not forget your prayers nor other religious duties
at any cost."

Though Maurice would remain a strict Catholic
throughout his life, he would manage to do it without
giving up his chosen career. He was bent on performing,
and he was determined to make his living as an actor;
what inspired him to this course remains a mystery.

Maurice had begun to get some good parts in stock
companies, and he was definitely on his way up when

friends introduced him to Mae Altschuh. Mae was a
"steady-eyed little blonde" nineteen years of age. "The
halo of romance around Maurice Costello's curls was
brighter than the gas flares lighting the American stage,"
their daughter Helene wrote about that magical time in
her parents' lives.

Mae Altschuh had been born in Brooklyn in 1882,
and she had been raised in the New York home of her
stepfather, English-born Vincent Tresham, who had defi-
nite ideas about proper behavior and made sure that Mae
observed his rules. Little is known about Mae's mother,
Katherine Callendar Altschuh Tresham. They led a life of
"quiet refinement." Maurice's friends were glamorous and
exciting in comparison to the people Mae met in Tresham's
house. Even though Mae was much more serious than
Maurice, she loved the vivacious Irish leading man and
would make a fair mate for him. Like many women at the
time, Mae had no aspirations for herself; she would find
no greater joy than to live through her husband—and
later through her children. In 1948, Helene Costello wrote
about her parents' meeting and marriage.

To Mr. Tresham, the stepfather, Maurice represented human vice and folly, because he came from "The Stage." Dad got such a cool reception on his first visit that he never returned as a guest. He knew where he wasn't wanted!

Mae, however, had fastened such a claim on his quixotic Irish heart in that one visit that he had to see her again.

For a whole spring they met secretly, to walk New York's windy streets arm in arm. One night, after Dad's last performance in his current engagement, they slipped around the corner to a near-by church and were married.

Dad was leaving early the next morning with a stock company, on tour, and they suddenly decided they couldn't stand the separation without a claim on each other. They kissed good-bye a block from her home. Mae went back to Tresham's house, and Dad hurried to the station to join the troupe.

He was gone almost a year.

He returned with a new wardrobe and with money in his pocket. More, he had seasoned and matured as an actor. He had gone away a rather wild but charming boy; he came back a tested artist, ready for the meteoric success which lay only a few years away.

He did not tell Mae he was coming home. The first she knew, there came a strong, violent pull of the bell cord. She ran from her room at the head of the stairs, her heart pounding because—well, none of the Tresham's friends ever yanked the bell like that! She knew!

Her stepfather went to the door.

"Sir," came a beloved voice—one trained to carry faultlessly to the highest galleries—"Sir, with your kind permission, I should like to speak with my wife."

It was not like Mae to run down into his arms. Instead, she returned quietly to her room.

When she came down a few moments later her bags were packed to travel, wherever Maurice wanted to take her. The sight of those bags made Tresham accept the truth that his little ewe lamb really had married "that actor fellow." He sighed as Mae went demurely into the protecting crook of Maurice's arm.

"Now that you're married, Costello, perhaps you'll settle down to a respectable job and give up this stage nonsense," he said.

Maurice's eyes blazed. Knowing his temper, and how his eyes would take fire when he got angry, I know exactly how he looked.

"Sir, I'll overlook your tradesman's background for the sake of my wife but don't presume too far!" he shouted.

(Well he claimed that was all he said! I have my doubts. When aroused, his vocabulary could halt all work at a ship's side and collect a rapt, admiring audience of teamsters and stevedores. Mr. Tresham was a hatter, to my father a contemptible mercantile man.)

After that outburst there was no chance of reconciliation. Mae went away with him that very evening.

Almost immediately two jobs offered themselves. One was a part in a good Broadway play. It would keep him before the New York public, and would permit him to make a home for Mae. The other was a tour with a repertory company, the school in which great actors were shaped. It paid better, too.

But what about his wife? He knew the one-a-day and loved it, but could he ask her to share its rough-and-tumble existence? If he did—would she?

She would.

Cold, dingy hotel bedrooms. Hot, stuffy ones. Meals at depot cafés. Red plush day coach seats. Towns and theaters in such rapid succession that she recalled them later like pickets on a fence all alike and close together.

But, she loved it because Maurice was with her. As for him, to know that she was in the audience or wings was inspiration.

Three months out of New York the troupe reached Buffalo. The night they were going to open there, Mae declared she didn't feel like going down to the theater, for the first time. Instead, she made a date with a physician, while Maurice went to the theater with a crony, another actor in the troupe.

When they arrived at the stage entrance they found it barred. The worst fate that could befall a travelling company was theirs. The manager had skipped, leaving them stranded.

All they had left were their clothes and a few personal costumes. Dad had not saved much. Neither had any other member of the troupe. They had all taken part of their pay in salary "chits," drawn on the vanished company treasurer.

Between them, Dad and his friend could raise $2.70, and they still had their hotel bill to pay. Downcast and worried, they went back to the hotel to break the news to Mother. She seemed to be feeling better. He noticed she was brighter the moment he entered the room. Gently, he told her their plight. She smiled "I'm afraid you'll have to do something, Dear," she said, "because you're going to be a father."

The bottomless pit yawned at Maurice's feet. He wanted a son more than anything else in the world. He was the last of the Costellos. After pondering a while, he suddenly shouted, "Got it, Got it!"

The idea that had come to him both shocked and attracted him. He drew his pal out into the hall, where his devout little wife could not hear and explained it.

That evening, two young men in clerical attire carrying religious emblems went from house to house. They said they were "working their way through the seminary" by selling the emblems for a dollar down, another dollar C.O.D.

By midnight there was enough to send Mae to Pittsburgh to Maurice's parents, after paying the hotel bill. With about $5, Dad and his friend set out in search of another travelling stock company working down south.

The clerical costumes—the last assets of the stranded troupe—had been pawned after serving their purpose. Not for years did Mae know where the much-needed money came from.

The clerical role, played on front porches, was one of Dad's greatest performances in his fifty-year acting career.

During the early years Maurice got his grounding by playing many roles in many stock companies, the way good actors learned their craft back then. His reviews were good, and he acted with nearly all of the well-known troupes. He was with the Boyle Stock Company in Nashville, Tennessee, when on September 17, 1903, Mae gave birth to a beautiful baby girl she named Dolores. That year Maurice would also play in the Blaker Stock Company out of New York, in the Gilmore Stock Company's production of Barbara Freitchie in Springfield, Illinois, and in Louisa Lane Drew's favorite vehicle, *School for Scandal*, with the Yorkville Theater Stock Company of New York City.

He worked with the Spooner Stock Company in October 1904, acting a role in Victorien Sardou's *La Tosca*, based on the play that broke Maurice Barrymore's heart. A playbill from Phoenix, Arizona, Tuesday, December 15, 1904, announces *Mrs. Temple's Telegram*, a farce in three acts by Frank Wyatt and William Morris, with Maurice Costello as Jack Temple. For several years Maurice played from coast to coast and back again, and Mae traveled with him and made their home wherever they landed.

MAURICE WAS INTERVIEWED by *Motion Picture* magazine after his career had waned and he was working as an extra in *Lady Eve* with Barbara Stanwyck and Henry Fonda.

Maurice explained that he did not seek out an opportunity to act in pictures; rather, his career began with a chance meeting on Broadway.

I was standing in front of the Hofbrau House. I had a year's contract in my pocket. A stage contract, of course, having been on the stage, in stock, since childhood. Larry Barber, a friend and stage director, happened to pass and saw me standing there. He stopped as if struck. He said: "Don't go away, Cos, I'll be right back." I said: "I'll be here." Presently he returned. He asked me to go with him to the office of Van Dyke Brooks. I knew Van, too, knew he was directing the new-fangled "attractions" called moving pictures. I'd seen a few of them in nickelodeons. Funny old things like magic-lantern slides with the jitters. People laughed at them but, I remember, I didn't laugh.

Brooks said to me, "Look, Cos, will you work in a motion picture?" I said, "My God, Van, not in those galloping tintypes!" I didn't laugh at them as others did, true. But we were proud in those days. Moreover, it was well known that theater managers threatened to blacklist actors who worked in movies. But Van said, "Come, now, you're young, you have a family, this is off-season in the theater. Isn't five dollars a day coming in better than five dollars a day going out?" I thought it over. I thought, Maybe no one will know! I said, "All right, Van, what's the plot?"

And that's how I went into pictures. Things haven't changed so much. Actors still go into movies for the dough. As I was leaving, Van said, "If it rains, we can't work, of course, but you'll receive fifty cents just for coming over." And that's what I did receive for my first day at the studio—fifty cents! In those days you got $2.50 if you just put your make-up on and it rained and you couldn't work. And if the handle of the camera so much as turned, you got your $5.00. I never used make-up until I became an extra. But I often made a pass with that powder puff just to get the $5.00.

"SO I WENT TO THE OLD Vitagraph Studio on the outskirts of Brooklyn. And my Great Days began. A.E. Smith and Commodore J. Stuart Blackton were the men at the helm...the first producers."

About this time Vitagraph's picture crew came to Sheepshead Bay to work on location. As usual, a crowd of spectators gathered behind the camera to watch the shooting of

Mae Aetshuh and Maurice Costello on their wedding day, June 8, 1902.

a moving picture. In that group of bystanders was Florence Turner, the daughter of an acting family who lived nearby. Miss Turner, as beautiful as any actress already employed by Vitagraph, impressed the crew, and shortly after, she was working at the studio in Flatbush with another unknown, Maurice Costello.

Maurice's "first appearance was before an old hand-cranked camera on the Vitagraph lot," Helene wrote. Maurice said he made so many films that he wasn't able to say which one was first. "But I think it was titled *The Foundling* and I know that Florence Turner was my leading lady." He also recalled that Van Dyke Brooks was his first director. We know he played the leading role in *The Adventures of Sherlock Holmes* in 1905. (In July 1910 a fire destroyed the negatives of every film the company had made, so filmographies are sometimes fuzzy.)

Though J. Stuart Blackton and Albert E. Smith were Englishmen, the story of their Vitagraph company is a thoroughly American tale. Blackton, who was working at the *New York Evening World* as a reporter and cartoonist, was sent to interview Thomas Edison about his new kinescope machine, which allowed viewers to see tiny

moving pictures by looking into the top of a small box and turning a crank. But Edison had something better to show Blackton that day, and Blackton immediately saw possibilities.

At this point, the viewing of moving pictures was a solitary pleasure—with one's face pressed to a viewing device, the experience could not be shared. Blackton had a talent for drawing, and he often perfomed by giving talks and sketching rapidly on large sheets of paper. A few lines here and there and the likeness of one celebrity changed into that of someone else. When Edison learned of Blackton's talent, he was delighted. He filmed one of Blackton's chalk talks, and by the time he left Blackton had placed an order for one of the first Edison Projecting Kinetoscopes. He had no idea how he would pay. Luckily for him, his friend Smith, also a vaudeville performer, saw the possibilities also and set out to help raise money. In 1886 they purchased the equipment and began to combine short moving pictures with their stage acts.

They took in another partner and began to make a name for capturing on film a number of major historical events (some real, at least one "reinacted") They covered

Portrait of Mae early in the Costello marriage.

the Spanish-American War, Teddy Roosevelt's Rough Riders in Cuba, the Boer War in South Africa. They produced a film of the Battle of Santiago by the creative use of miniatures. They filmed the assassination of McKinley, the inauguration of Teddy Roosevelt, and scenes of San Francisco after the great earthquake of 1906. They were the first company to film Mark Twain, one of the most popular entertainers of his day, telling one of his stories. Audiences were hungry to view scenes of far-off locales and current events.

By 1906, the art of film had became sophisticated compared to the inauspicious beginnings of the industry. Audiences were no longer willing to pay money simply to watch movement—they demanded stories. People were employed to write scenarios, special studios were built—some, like Edison's Black Mariah, made to turn with the sun—and actors were learning to how their stage skills

translated to celluloid and improving their technique for the new medium. "I don't know exactly how to give you the feeling of what it was to be a star in those days," Maurice explained. "It was a pioneer feeling, I'd say.... We were young, we were blazing a new trail in the entertainment world, we were in at the birth of a new, great industry. I can't say that I knew how great it would be, how big, but I can say that I sensed a lusty, growing thing. If I hadn't, I wouldn't have given up the stage. Yes, I did foresee a future. Not my future, thank God, but a future for what we then referred to, tongue in cheek, as 'galloping tintypes.'"

Maurice was intelligent and outspoken and turned out to be a stubborn leader in the process of hammering out early movie procedures. On Maurice's first movie assignment he took a stand that changed working conditions for actors. He was shocked to find out that actors and actresses were not free to concentrate on their craft but were pressed into service as carpenters, set dressers, scene painters, and wardrobe mistresses. Perhaps because he was used to the strict code of behavior in the theater, he expected the same courtesies as an actor before the camera—and he demanded them. Helene wrote,

> J. Stuart Blackton, one of the Vitagraph founders, was directing that day. When Dad reported for work he found the whole cast banging away with saws and hammers, knocking scenery and props together.
>
> Blackton handed him a claw hammer and said, "Here, Mr. Costello. Lend a hand. The sooner we start, the sooner we're through."
>
> Holding the loathsome tool as if it were a dueling pistol, Dad sighted down the handle at a fellow actor who was sheepishly sawing away at a board.
>
> "I am an actor," he said, "not a blasted carpenter!"
>
> He threw the hammer across the room. Blackton ducked it. Dad was close to being fired from pictures before he ever went to work.
>
> Then, one by one, the others laid down their tools. Their artistic integrity had suddenly risen. Besides, it was hard work! Blackton tore his hair, but he ended by sending out for a brace of experienced stage carpenters.
>
> The revolt spread swiftly and soon other studios had to hire carpenters and stagehands as the artists threw away their tools.

Maurice "first worked in pictures anonymously, like every other stage actor," Helene wrote. "They paid well but the flickering thriller-diller one reelers were beneath the dignity of a serious actor—then." The studios didn't want the public to know the names of their performers because they realized that players would be able to command higher salaries if they became "personalities." And "legitimate" stage actors and actresses sometimes didn't want their names advertised in connection with movies anyway. Consequently, players became known by their attributes. Biograph had Mary Pickford, "the girl with the curls," and Vitagraph boasted Maurice Costello, "the man with the dimples," and Florence Turner "the Vitagraph girl." Later Lillian Walker would become the company's female "Dimples."

By then Maurice's pictures were being shown in theaters, and he was being noticed. He was handsome, with dark-lashed eyes, a strong smile, and those dimples. "Every day the Vitagraph office shipped him a bale of adoring fan letters addressed simply to 'Dimples,'" Helene wrote. "Maurice knew that his dimples were real assets. So were fans. For a whole month he brooded over that phenomenal mail—for fan mail, as we know it, just didn't exist in those days." Maurice said, "In those days all letters written to me aimed at one point: 'Who are you?' they all asked, 'What is your name?' I kept hounding A.E. Smith to give us screen credit. They didn't want to because they were afraid we would become too popular and ask for too much money."

Again Maurice used the method of head-on confrontation that had worked so well when he was expected to build his own sets for Blackton. "Finally, after my fifth picture, I delivered an ultimatum: I said: 'Unless my name goes on the screen with my next release, next Thursday, I am going back to my first love, the theater.'" Helene wrote, "Clear up to his 11 A.M. deadline the deadlock continued, but Vitagraph capitulated—because they had seen and appraised the mail to 'Dimples,' too." "That did it," Maurice recounted. "For a few days later I was told: 'Cos, your name goes on the screen and, from now on you will star in all productions!' That was how names first went on the screen. And that was how the First Star was born. That was the birth, actually, of the 'star system.' Why, if it hadn't been for me, you might be calling Gable 'What-a-Man,' and nothing else but!"

While Maurice was making a name for himself, Mae was standing behind him. Maurice prayed for a son to carry on his family line, and Mae wanted very much to oblige her husband. On June 21, 1906, she gave birth, with difficulty, to a second daughter, Helen, who would soon become Helene. If it was any consolation to Maurice, he had produced two of the most beautiful children in the world—and the most photogenic. Dark Helen complimented her golden sister. Both girls were destined to carry on the acting tradition begun by their father. While they were still quite young they would become the first child stars of the Vitagraph company, and they would frequently play in their father's productions.

In 1908, Maurice made nine films, including *Ex-Convict No. 900, The Dancer and the King: A Romantic Story of Spain, Slippery Jim's Repentance, Salome, Leah the Forsaken,* and several full-length Shakespearean productions. For a former stage actor used to playing the same role night after night and being ever ready to act any one of a dozen parts at the drop of a hat, producing a little fewer than one film a month probably did not tax him all that much. "We weren't pampered in those days," Maurice said.

It wasn't a cushy job, being a star in the early 1900s. The luxury-standard came later, unfortunately, I think, for all of us. Actors, like all men, work better when they are conscious of their bellies. But we were pioneers and pioneering is never easy. I was an all-around athlete. Whatever the script called for, I did it. We had no stand-ins, no doubles. We were our own stunt men. When I think of the crazy chances I took, the fights under water, the horses I rode, the falls and climbs.

I look a the stars today, snug in their padded, portable dressing rooms, while stunt men risk their lives and limbs to the glory of the star, I have to laugh. When we went on location in those days, we just went short distances, down on Long Island, over to Staten Island. We traveled by trolley-car and ferry boat. We carried our lunch-boxes with us. We had to or we didn't eat. We all doubled in brass.

"DOUBLING IN BRASS" meant to work in more than one capacity. Though Maurice had taken a stand against working as a stage hand, he did not always object to wearing more than one hat at Vitagraph. "I directed many of my pictures as well as acted in them," he recalled. "Florence Turner used to pay off the actors after her day's work before the camera was done. At the end of the day, she would stand there with the pay roll, doling it out. She paid me my first wages in this business. Imagine how a Hedy Lamarr or a Marlene Dietrich would look, dispensing the day's wages to a Gable or a Boyer." Norma Talmage, when she began at Vitagraph, doubled as the wardrobe mistress.

The pace of production continued. In 1909, Maurice made sixteen pictures, including *The Galley Slave, The Way of the Cross, The Gift of Youth,* and *The Plot That Failed.* He played Lysander in *A Midsummer Night's Dream,* David in *Saul and David,* and Jean Valjean in *Les Misérables.*

Maurice liked to recount his "firsts," and the year 1911 held a number of them for the Costello family. *Motion Picture* magazine made its debut in 1911, with Maurice and his dimples on the cover of the first issue, and Vitagraph began publishing *Life Portrayals* that same year, giving their top male star plenty of press. These early entertainment magazines exploited fans' insatiable interest in the careers and private lives of the stars and used the stars to sell products and endorse businesses. They listed schedules and appearances so that fans could catch

their favorite players, either on the screen or in person. "My first interview, first gallery portraits, first stills were published in the first fan magazine, *Motion Picture,*" Maurice said. "We began together, *Motion Picture* and I. I won the first Popularity Contest ever run, also in *Motion Picture.*"

Another first for the family was that Mae played the role of the nurse in *Her Crowning Glory.* Then Maurice, whose Masonic association was very important to him, became a life member of the Constitution Chapter of the Masons on December 5th, 1911. He would count that as a major achievement in his life. Mae appreciated this accomplishment too; her maternal grandfather, John Callendar, had become a 32nd degree Mason in a ceremony in Scotland along with the Prince of Wales.

The film that Maurice considered his best work was also released in 1911. "*A Tale of Two Cities* was my masterpiece," he said. "As Clark Gable may well say *Gone with the Wind* is his masterpiece, so *A Tale of Two Cities* was mine." Florence Turner played the female lead to Maurice's Sidney Carton, and they were supported by Vitagraph's popular comedian John Bunny, Julia Swayne Gordon, Ralph Ince, and Lillian Walker. The film is also remembered for containing Norma Talmage's screen debut as a woman on the way to the guillotine. William Humphreys directed the forty-minute film, the first filmed version of Dickens's classic tale.

These were Maurice's "Great Days," as he called them.

> In the early days, my competitors were Arthur Johnson, Guy Combs, Henry B. Walthall, Bronco Billy Anderson....We were the Gable, Taylor, Gene Autry, Power of our day. Earle Williams came in later. Billy Anderson was, I think, the first of the stars to foreshadow the way Hollywood stars were to live later on, with their mansions and swimming pools and polo ponies. Billy had a limousine, I remember, equipped with every comfort of the most palacial home, including hot and cold running water! I had my huge estate on Long Island, my private yacht anchored in the basin, my fleet of high-powered cars—and servants. My family wanted for nothing, could think of nothing to want....We ushered in the fabulous way of life of the Swansons, Wally Reids, Bebe Daniels and others with their huge extravagances, huge salaries....Yes, those were the days when I was the whole smoke, when the Costellos were beginning to be known (my young daughters and I) as the Royal Family of the Screen.

During his "Great Days" Maurice collected automobiles.

Maurice in one of his
best-known early roles
as the Yellow Kid.

IN DECEMBER 1912, a group of Vitagraph players, including Maurice Costello and family, left on a scouting trip around the world. With the Costellos were, among others, James and Clara Kimball Young, Vitagraph's head of the scenario department, and cameraman Harry Keepers. By this time Maurice was directing as well as starring in films; he held the film rights to Jules Verne's *Around the World in Eighty Days,* and he was on the lookout for locations for that production.

The trip originally was planned for the purpose of making pictures on a world tour, but it made an about face when the movie fans around the world received the news that I was on the way! That was my first trip out of the United States and Canada, and it was the first opportunity these outsiders were presented to see me in the palpitating flesh. It was surprising to me, how many of the foreign countries, Japan, China, Egypt, where they speak little or any English at all, the natives knew their movies well enough to spot me in a crowd, and come clamoring about in delirious worship.

When they sailed on the 13th, both Mae and Dolores became seasick. By the second day, "storm doors all let down, rough and choppy sea. Waves reach above port holes, almost to second deck." At this point most of the party was sick. By the 16th, skies had cleared, and they began shooting on shipboard. They completed seventeen scenes, though Maurice noted "light not the best."
The ship arrived in Honolulu for a twelve-hour stop, and they celebrated Christmas on board as they shoved off from Hawaii. The day was like summer, but Maurice dressed as Santa Claus. After he made his appearance, they

The Costello family home in Bayside, Long Island.

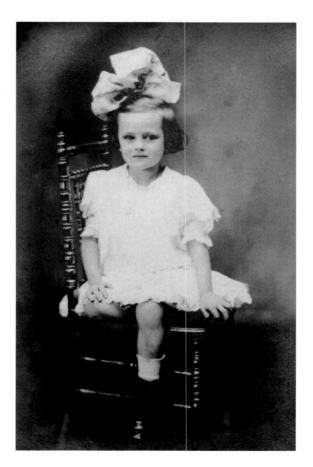

Helene Costello at the camera.

Dolores Costello was beautiful even as a young child.

The Costello girls with their pets.

enjoyed a Japanese play and wrestling matches. "Mrs. Cos gave me a pair of cuff buttons," Maurice noted.

The troupe traveled from place to place, shooting in exotic settings and on shipboard. They made a number of films, including *Fellow Voyagers, Lesson in Botany, Perplexed Bridegroom, Joys of a Jealous Wife, Hindoo Charm,* and *Spirit of the Orient.* As the films were finished and in the can, they were sent on to Vitagraph's London office, where they were to be developed for worldwide distribution. This plan did not work out all that well.

On March 18th, they were on the train to Bombay. Maurice noted that it was "hot as Hell." The next day, they stopped at the Taj Mahal Hotel, and on March 20 Wedding Eve at the Botanical Gardens. "Very pretty," Maurice wrote. "Went through native quarters. Family getting along."

Costello thought to record how the family was getting along, because many times on the trip they were not. The discomfort of the varied climates took its toll on dispositions; they were too uncomfortable to work. Jealousies and tension cropped up from spending so much time in close quarters with the same group of people. Some days the wives refused to work. By the time they reached Cairo, Mae and Maurice were barely speaking.

In Cairo, the company filmed *Moses* on the bank of the Nile, then went on to Luxor to scout locations. When they returned from Thebes they found a cable that told them not to make the Moses film. "Big loss," Maurice wrote in his diary.

They completed their business in Egypt, filming by the pyramids and the Sphinx, then they traveled on from Port Said to Italy. They made some location shots in Italy, but the weather refused to cooperate. The government officials, however, rolled out the red carpets for the Vitagraph troupe, and they attended many theater parties studded with minor dignitaries.

In Rome, Maurice was overwhelmed with the welcome he received. He was met by a huge crowd of adoring fans, which was to him "the biggest thrill," he recalled. "The Italian population, judging from my name, believed me to be Italian, whereas, in reality I am part Irish and Spanish. The Roman Italian is a charming person, and the reception of one contingent of Italians to another supposed Italian was my own personal thrill, even while they were having theirs."

Because of the Italian's great affection for him, Maurice and Mae nearly lost their children in the hotel in Rome. "The Romans were particularly thorough in their presenta-tion of flowers to us. No matter where I went, there were flowers. Corners were filled with them, every street I trav-eled was strewn with their petals. One day, the Italian hosts of mine piled the flowers so high in our suite of rooms, we lost the two children among them, and barely managed to recover them from a complete case of nausea. You know, too many flowers do become nauseating!"

When Maurice arrived in London, he received a letter from Albert E. Smith, treasurer of the Vitagraph Company. "My Dear Cos," Smith wrote, "I suppose the reason that you did not get all the letters I wrote while you were away was because I only wrote them in my mind." Smith explained that the developed film from the London office had just arrived in New York and that the negatives were still tied up in the Customs. Though the players had thought that their films were being released in the States, the travelers actually reached New York shortly after their handiwork did.

IN 1915 MAE PLAYED Mrs. King in *When a Woman Loves,* and she had roles in two movies in 1917, *The Money Mill* (as Mrs. King) and *Her Right to Live* (as Mrs. Biggs). She acted under the name "Mrs. Maurice Costello," which is exactly how she thought of herself at that time—as Maurice's spouse and helpmate, and mother to his children.

This was the year that Maurice left Vitagraph and "the down-grade began." The company would last only a few more years before it was sold to Warner Brothers. Maurice found freelance jobs. "The War came and there was not much doing. I had a big estate on my hands, not enough coming in for maintenance. In 1922 and '23, I did a cou-ple of pictures for Paramount." Then, as Ethel Barrymore would rely on *The Twelve Pound Look* to get her through periods of little work, Maurice began to tour in a playlet he liked called *The Payoff.* He would perform at vaudeville theaters and on double bills with films. He traveled all over the country with this piece, discontinuing his tour when a film part presented itself, then picking it up where he left off when he didn't have movie work.

IN THE EARLY 1920S, Maurice, Mae and the girls trav-eled to Miami to work with Famous Players-Laskey on Edith Wharton's *Glimpses of the Moon.* Dolores, who was seventeen at this time, had the part of an ingenue. She and Helene were resuming their acting careers; they had shone brightly as children, but they had sat out the past

158

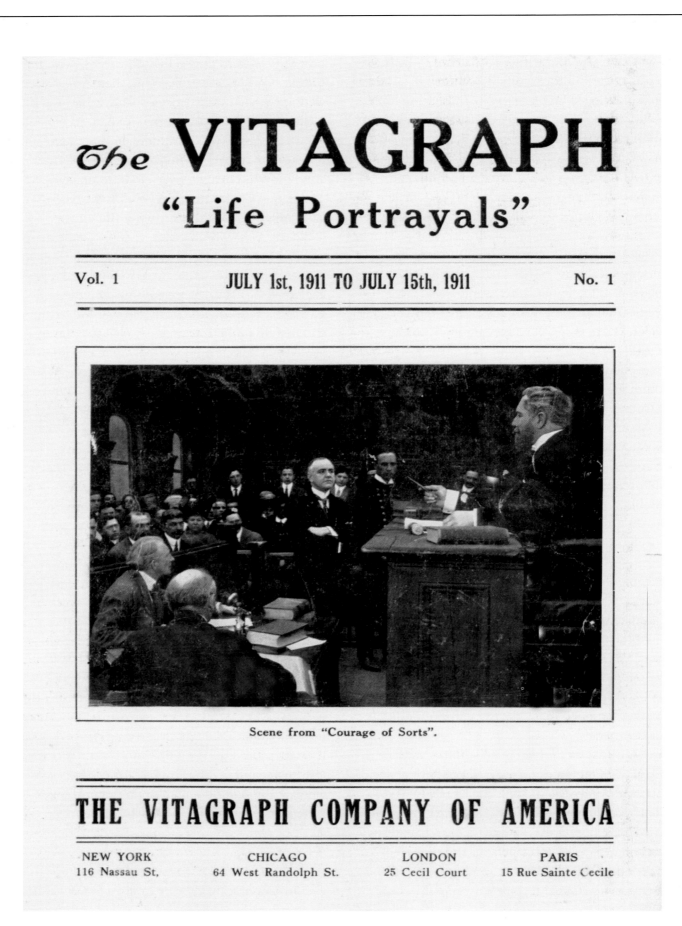

Maurice was interviewed in the first issue of *The Vitagraph "Life Portrayals"* in 1911.

few years, what Louisa Drew had called "that unhappy age" when one is "not a child and certainly not a woman."

By 1924, Dolores and Helene had been hired by George White Scandals as a sister act. Mae traveled with them from Philadelphia to Cincinnati to Detroit and Chicago. As Eliza Kinlock had insisted when young Louisa was on the stage, they were never without a chaperon. Among the many admirers of the Costello girls was James Montgomery Flagg, the illustrator. He was so enamored of Dolores's poise and grace that he had her pose for him on a number of occasions. Her likeness appeared frequently in illustrations to stories in popular magazines.

The girls were seen by a Warner Brothers' scout, who pursued them tirelessly to sign studio contracts and come to Los Angeles. Helene wanted to remain on the legitimate stage and develop her acting career. She dreamed of becoming a comedienne. Dolores, however, was more persuasive with Mae, Helene relented, and Warner Brothers signed the Costello girls. Maurice and Mae were going their own ways by this time. They maintained contact by letter when Mae traveled to the West Coast with the girls.

Dolores and Helene were getting bit parts and walk-ons. Though they didn't realize it yet, Dolores was on the brink of her big break.

BARNEY GLAZER interviewed Maurice on his radio show in 1936, shortly after the completion of *Hollywood Boulevard*, which was billed as his comeback role. Francis X. Bushman, Mae Marsh, and other experienced players were also "coming back" in the film. Maurice was on the radio show to publicize the Associated Cinema Stars organization, the purpose of which was "to perpetuate the names of those who have aided in the progress of motion pictures, to provide a meeting place for the entertainment of members and their friends. And, to promote in every way their social, artistic, and material welfare. Those men and women, you will readily understand, planned and established the Hollywood of today. Without them, there would be neither the entertainment nor business centers of the town of Hollywood. The entire world owes them a vote of thanks," Maurice said. He must have been think-

ing about himself as he described the contributions that had been made by the old-timers. He was no longer on top of the entertainment world.

"In 1927 I did a picture with Ken Manard," Maurice said. "The Actor's strike in 1929 didn't do me any good, I'd been Equity for years. I was walking downstairs, and I knew it." Maurice did what he knew how to do: He kept working, as did many of the leading actors and actresses of the bygone era of silent film. "I became an extra. Now and then I get bit parts. In *Mr. Smith Goes to Washington*, in *Little Bit of Heaven*, in *Third Finger, Left Hand*. For the most part I am an extra." Imagine the experienced actor feeling out of his league in front of the camera. "At first I was timid," Maurice said. "I was afraid of doing something wrong. There are more damn tricks to this game of extra-ing than there are to starring. Now I get a hell of a bang out of it." Did Maurice hope to make it back to the top? "If it comes again, it will come," he said. "I don't care anymore. I don't hope for anything except the ability to keep my head above water. Every night I thank God I've got my health and strength. Every night I pray I can go on, even in this little way. I don't regret any of it."

Throughout Maurice's career, he was more than just a fine actor and director. He involved himself in union organizing for bettering the working conditions of all the Hollywood trades. He was a founder of The Green Room and on the board that developed the Motion Picture Home in Malibu, which was established to serve those in the profession who were ill or needed a residence upon retirement. The Costello Theater on Broadway at 159th Srteet was built in his honor. "So I was the First Star," he mused. "I was also responsible for having the players' names put on the screen. I was responsible for slower motion in pictures. I helped the 'tintypes' to cease their galloping, to slow down to natural motion. I can't say that I wouldn't like to be young again. I would, of course I would. I can't say that I don't wish I were Clark Gable, Robert Taylor, up at the top again, as they are. But in my heart, I don't envy them so much. I don't regret I was a star when the industry was very young. For we didn't only play parts in those days. We were part of the whole thing. We helped to build it and mould it and make it."

On December 7, 1912, Vitagraph sent a party of players and technicians on a round-the-world cruise. Pictured at the Temple of Luxor, travelers included W.S. Smith and his wife, Clara Kimball Young and her husband James Young, William V. Ramous and his wife, Maurice and Mae Costello and their two children, Helene and Dolores, Eugene Mullin, manager of the Vitagraph scenario department, and cameraman Harry Keepers.

Mae, Dolores, and Helene in Kamakura, Japan.

The streets of Rangoon, Burma.

In front of the Rajah's house in Calcutta.

The cast and crew in Calcutta, India, where they filmed *The Hindoo Charm* (1913).

More Calcutta scenes.

The Costellos in Bombay, India.

In Luxor, Egypt.

In Cairo, Egypt.

Dolores and Helene in Venice, Italy.

Leaving Venice on the *Train De Lux*.

The Costellos on a motoring trip in one of Maurice's cars.

Maurice dressed for a
stage role as a dapper
Englishman.

The Costello family in Miami for the filming of *Glimpses of the Moon* (1923).

Dolores and Helene Costello in a beauty contest.

Dolores and Helene Costello at the time they were signed by Warner Brothers.

Dolores Costello, Warner Brothers starlet.

Dolores Costello in a scene from *Glorious Betsy* (1928).

Dolores Costello, starring
in Warner Brothers'
The Third Degree (1926).

More scenes from
Glorious Betsy (1928).

Dolores in Warner Brothers'
Noah's Ark, as Mary (left) and
Miriam (below).

After the Honeymoon

For an actress to be a success she must have the face of Venus, the brains of Minerva, the grace of Terpsichore, the memory of Macaulay, the figure of Juno, and the hide of a rhinoceros.

—ETHEL BARRYMORE

WHAT HAPPENED TO the children of the Great Barrymore? For the two who chose the family business, life was often difficult. Today we are more aware of the dangers faced by child stars, but decades ago the attitude was often unsympathetic: *These children have everything they could ever want, and still they can't behave themselves.*

Diana Joan Blyth Barrymore, Jack Barrymore's daughter with his second wife Michael Strange, became an actress. Her beginning was auspicious. At eighteen, she was invited by David O. Selznick to make a screen test for the role of Scarlett O'Hara. Unimpressed, he advised her to try her luck on the stage and to keep in touch.

She was introduced to polite society a few months later at a debutante ball in New York, and Cholly Knickerbocker reported that she was "the personality girl of the season." She spent a year at the American Academy of Dramatic Arts, and in the late 1930s she opened in summer theater stock as an apprentice. Her name no doubt opened that door, but it was in Maine, not Hollywood. Her reviews were lukewarm, and Jack wrote to the critic, applauding Diana for trying to learn her trade. "Nobody gets to be a star overnight," he pointed out.

Though both of her parents were strikingly attractive, Diana was somewhat plain, with a rounded face and large cheeks. All of her life she felt the strain of being less than classically beautiful. Her uncle Lionel could have told her the joys of being a character actor, the fun of playing the roles with the most meat and the most opportunity for showing off one's talent, but he was strangely withdrawn from the girl. And Jack himself could have explained how he enjoyed roles that allowed him to alter his handsome exterior and stretch his acting ability.

Wisely, Ethel pointed out that too much was being expected of the younger Barrymores. They were not being offered the "tray carrying" roles that her Uncle Jack had given her; instead they were given large roles and were expected to carry a production when they hadn't had the years of practice that Lionel, Ethel, and Jack had been allowed.

Jack had, for presumably noble reasons, relinquished all claim on his daughter to former wife Michael Strange, and Diana saw him only a few times during her childhood. At boarding school she made up colorful and detailed stories about her father and his Hollywood friends even though she did not use the Barrymore name and eventually had to sneak into a matinee to see him for the first time on the screen. Ironically, that first film was *A Bill of Divorcement*. A complex swirl of conflicting emotions engulfed Diana as she watched her father meet an on-screen daughter he had not seen since she was a child.

Diana Barrymore, Jack's older daughter, and John Boles in Universal's *Between Us Girls* (1942).

An ad for *Between Us Girls*, a dream role for an experienced actress. The part was too complex for Diana, who did her best to play a twelve-year-old girl, Joan of Arc, Sadie Thompson, and Queen Victoria.

Diana Barrymore with Brian Donlevy in *Nightmare* (1942).

In 1942, the year that Jack Barrymore died, Diana married Bramwell Fletcher, an actor seventeen years her senior. Fletcher had played Billee in *Svengali* with Jack in the title role, and he had also played a small uncredited role in *A Bill of Divorcement*. Fletcher and his wife never acted on film together, and after a period of about five years the couple divorced. In 1950, a month before her mother died, Diana married Robert Wilcox, an actor eleven years older than she was. They played together in stage productions but their performances together were never recorded on film. Their marriage lasted about the same length of time as did Diana's first union.

In 1957 Diana wrote a tell-all book about the heartache of her childhood and early life. *Too Much, Too Soon* was in some ways a cry for help, and the book turned out to be a best seller. However, the damage was already done, and Diana died young, unable to enjoy her success.

JOHN AND DOLORES' DAUGHTER, Dolores Ethel Mae "Dede" Barrymore, lost her interest in acting after she tried a role in a junior college production, and her decision was later reinforced by an unwanted invitation onto the casting couch of an unnamed studio executive. At age twenty-two Dede married Thomas Fairbanks, son of an exile from Vienna who had once chaired the department of voice at the conservatory there. The couple had one child, son Antony John Barrymore Fairbanks, who spent his formative years at his grandmother's home, the avocado ranch in Fallbrook. His uncle John says that he helped raise Tony after the boy's parents divorced, and his cousin Johnny calls him the "real Barrymore," the one who would make a good swashbuckler. Now an adult, he has developed an intense interest in the family business. And this interest has been passed on to his daughter, Samantha, who is studying for the theater.

JOHN DREW BARRYMORE, Jack's only son, became interested in acting as a teenager, but he could not convince his mother that the idea had merit. He was still young, and Dolores knew what Hollywood could do to a boy. Frustrated, John ran away, intending to pursue his dream—only to be recognized and detained at the airport before he could make good his escape. "I guess he was born to act," Dolores said. She ceased trying to keep him from the thing he said he most wanted to do.

From the first day of his career, Barrymore Junior suffered from comparisons to his famous father. His Barrymore mannerisms must have been innate, for he remembered seeing his father only once the entire time he was growing up. John Drew was handsome in a intensely exciting way—black, shiny hair and glittering blue eyes, and that walk that must have come from Maurice Barrymore, who was said to have taught American actors to swagger on the stage. He also had the Barrymore flair for expressing his attitude by the subtle movement of an eyebrow. In some ways he was more handsome than his father, and his acting had an intensity that came from deep inside.

John's first movie was *The Sundowners* (1950), with Robert Preston. As little brother Jeff Cloud he sizzled, though he was not satisfied with the performance he'd turned in. Comparisons to his father inevitably followed. Like his half sister Diana, John would see his first Jack Barrymore movie when he was a teenager. Unlike Diana, who sat breathless as she watched her handsome father, John was completely disconcerted. "I was shocked at seeing the similarity of his expressions and gestures to mine," he said.

Next for John was another western, *High Lonesome* (1950), for which he pulled top billing and further comparison to his famous father. At an age when Jack had been walking on in roles that called for a handsome face and a couple of lines, his son was being asked to carry whole productions—before he was old enough to vote. In nearly every interview he expressed his desire to be himself and find his own way. Ironically, had Jack been in his son's life he might have been able to help—he had been compared with his father all of his life too.

After a brief stint on the stage, John worked with director Joe Losey on *The Big Night*. This could have been the young star's best performance yet, but in 1950 Losey came under investigation by the House Un-American Activities Committee. Rather than testify at the witch hunt, Losey fled the country, leaving two underlings to finish the editing on his latest film. Instead of a movie of real substance, what ended up on screen was a story cut beyond all recognition.

In *While the City Sleeps* (1956) John found a role that suited his growing intensity, and he was given star billing. His anger and energy enhanced the character of Robert Manners, a murderer who derives his desire to kill from reading comic books. John would do his best early acting in roles that allowed him to express his troubled side. He excelled in *Never Love a Stranger* (1958), a gritty tale of a mobster pitted against his childhood friend, now a district attorney (Steve McQueen in his film debut), and in *High School Confidential* (1958), where he played one of his most memorable roles as J.I. Coleridge, a hood with a smooth southern accent.

In 1952 John had married the hot-tempered actress Cara Williams, and their marital battles were often publicized on both sides of the Atlantic. While fighting, extricating himself from legal scrapes, and repeatedly breaking up and then reuniting with his red-headed wife, John produced an heir, John Barrymore III. But by 1958 John and Cara had divorced and John had left for Italy. He had always loved Europe, remembering his days of study at the Paris Conservatoire and the Comedie Francaise. There he hoped to make a name for himself on his own merits.

In the early sixties Europe, and Italy in particular, was thick with Hollywood expatriates, including such well-known names as Esther Williams, Guy Madison, and Anita Ekberg. Some had moved there to take advantage of the weather or the atmosphere, but most had come to get work. John made a number of films in Rome, including *The Cossacks, I'll See You in Hell, Daggers of Blood,* and *Pontius Pilate*. In *The Night They Killed Rasputin* he even played the same role his father had perfected in *Rasputin and the Empress*. John's movies were shown in Italy, Spain, and Yugoslavia, and some were dubbed for English audiences.

On October 28, 1960, at the Church of Saint Sebastiano in his second year in Rome, John married film starlet Gabriella Palozzoli, and in 1962 Gaby and John had a daughter, Blyth. But by that time Gaby and John were not getting along. Their marriage was breaking up.

Returning to the United States in 1964, John turned to television. His creativity had flourished in 1957 on *Playhouse 90*, where he had hosted, acted, and directed with flair. He was rewarded with his own star on Hollywood Boulevard, near the entryway to the Hollywood Roosevelt Hotel. John appeared on *Gunsmoke* and the *Wild, Wild West* in 1965, and in 1967 he played the "bad guy" on the TV version of *Winchester 73*. His performances

John Drew Barrymore
in early publicity shots.

John Drew Barrymore in *Quebec* (1951)

John Drew Barrymore with Barbara Rush in *Quebec*.

John Blyth Barrymore III and his father.

John Drew Barrymore's first wife, Cara Williams, mother of John Barrymore III.

John Drew Barrymore and Betty Garret in *The Shadow on the Window* (1957).

John Drew Barrymore made films in Italy that were distributed in several countries. This lobby card advertises *I'll See You in Hell* with Eva Bartok (1965).

John Drew Barrymore's silver hair looks particularly appropriate in his role as Aderbad in *War of the Zombies* or *Night Star, Goddess of Electra* (1965).

John met Krishnamurti (a friend of his father's) in an airport, and the experience changed his life.

on *Rawhide* won him an award from the Western Heritage Center. The work he did in 1974 with David Carradine (son of John Carradine, a close friend of John Barrymore Sr.) in the *Kung Fu* series was some of his best. In this series Hollywood had the opportunity to see the sons of two great fathers and two great friends carry on the family tradition through two generations, as John was joined by his son John III, then a teenager, in several sequences.

Later John "Johnny" Barrymore III did some stage work, appearing in *Aria de Cappa* by Edna St. Vincent Millet and a remake of *The Jest*, which had been preformed years earlier by his grandfather and his Great Uncle Lionel. In the mid-1980s Johnny abandoned stage and screen after winning his fight against the family curse, leaving for a career in computer technology. He does not discount the possibility of doing further work in the entertainment field, and his rich Barrymore voice can be heard today in voice-overs on *Xena* and *Hercules*.

The last movie John Drew Barrymore made was *The Clones* (1974), an independent film directed by Paul Hunt involving numerous chase scenes through high weeds, up and down hallways, and through eerie sets and blinking lights meant to represent labs and scientific equipment. According to cameraman Michael Ferris, the director abandoned the film partway through, and John created dialog for the rest of the shoot. By shoving a "poor man's dolly" through the halls of Cal Tech using the widest lens they could find, the crew was able to get "really good visuals" without excessive expenditures. *The Clones* is not widely known today, but for Barrymore fans, John's cameo performance as an aging hippie is endearing. His classic profile is still attractive, and his rich voice, with its rolling *r*'s and a snippet of a British accent, reminds us of things past. The movie holds moments of real entertainment.

IN THE EARLY 1970s, Ildiko Jaid, nee Mako, aspiring actor, met John Barrymore Jr. and was instantly attracted to him. He was very handsome and "movie starrish" to her. She also found him highly intelligent and incredibly talented. John was bitter by this time, and he buried his pain in alcohol and drugs. He lashed out at everyone, particularly authority figures and loved ones. When she finally left him in 1975, Ildiko took with her the promise of the child she carried, which she said John wanted even more than she did. This child was, of course, Drew Barrymore. On the edge of this strange and tangled family, Drew could not hope to grow up without contention. But as difficult as her life was at certain points, she seems now to exhibit the positive attributes of her ancestors.

Drew was so adorable that the camera soon became the child's best friend. In 1977 Ildiko took her to audition for a Gaines Puppy Choice commercial. Hundreds of other cute kids were waiting for the same opportunity. But they didn't have the same stuff as this child with centuries of acting genes behind her. They sat her down on the floor and let loose a puppy, who ran immediately for Drew. When she reached out for it, the pup promptly nipped her on the nose. As Drew tells it, the onlookers gasped, probably thinking "lawsuit," but the toddler tipped back her head and laughed out loud. She got the part.

Lionel Barrymore rejected the idea of talent being passed down through the genes. He said that if his father had been a plumber, he and John would have followed in those footsteps. But if there is any doubt as to genetic influence on acting talent, one only has to look at Drew to find an example to support the theory. She knew very early that she wanted to be an actor, and she pushed her mother and herself until her dream was fulfilled. It must have been, as Dolores Costello said of her son, in the blood. Drew emulated relatives she had never heard of: her great-great grandmother Louisa Lane Drew, who made her first appearance on stage as an infant; her great grandmother Georgie Drew Barrymore, beautiful and witty, who began her career as a teen; her great aunt Ethel Barrymore, who staged her own performance of *Camille* at the age of ten and began her professional work at the age of fourteen; and her grandmother Dolores Costello, who, along with her sister, played child roles at Vitagraph during the early 1900s. The fact that she didn't know of these people didn't stop her from feeling the same need to perform.

Drew's first big part was in *E.T.–The Extra-Terrestrial*, a fantasy about a boy who befriends an alien. When she met director Steven Spielberg, a big kid himself, she beguiled him with descriptions of her fantasy punk band and musical lifestyle. She was adorable at that age: chipmunk cheeks and a slight lisp. Spielberg loved her immediately. "She just blew me away," he said. "There was no second choice. Drew Barrymore was the first choice for this part." Drew fell in love with Spielberg in return. And because she had such a flexible imagination, she fell in love with little E.T. too, worried about him when she wasn't working and had her lunch with him when she was. The entire production, including Drew Barrymore as little Gertie, has captivated audiences since the film was released in 1982. She also starred in *Irreconcilable Differences* (1984) and *Firestarter* (1984).

As a child, her talents had brought her very good roles. As she entered adolescence, the roles decreased and she fell prey to the social ills of our time, always accelerated in Hollywood. Caught up in the Hollywood party scene and given little parental oversight, Drew's addictions to alcohol and drugs spiraled out of control. She was in and out of therapy and rehabilitation programs for several years, and when she finally managed to beat her addictions, she did so in a courageous and public way. In her autobiography, *Little Girl Lost: A Child Star's Descent Into Addiction and Out Again*, written at the age of fourteen, she bares her soul and reveals her unflattering behavior as well as her successes. And when she speaks in interviews about her wild past, she does not apologize—she survived and she is proud of it. She matured into a well-spoken, compassionate young woman.

In the few past years, she's appeared in *Scream*, the popular horror film produced by Cary Wood and Cathy Conrad, and in Woody Allen's *Everybody Says I Love You*, a "take you back to the fifties" musical.

In 1998, she starred in *Ever After*, a Cinderella story with a twist. Her film *The Wedding Singer* (1998), grossed $55 million. And now the most sensational film of hers to date, *Charlie's Angels* (2000), has lifted Drew and her company even higher in Hollywood circles. As producer, Drew was instrumental in attracting Cameron Diaz to the project. Since its release, the action-packed film has earned over $125 million. Now twenty-six, Drew has emerged from her troubled youth with a new determination and what seems to be a completely positive outlook on life. Add that to her inborn talent, natural beauty, and unique style, and you have a package that combines all that has been great about the Lanes, the Drews, and the Barrymores. If the Barrymores are the history of Hollywood, perhaps Drew is its future.

Drew Barrymore and her mother Ildiko Jaid Mako Barrymore.

Drew's role as Gertie in *E.T.* brought her instant success in Hollywood and throughout the world—she even toured Japan. Here she poses with an E.T. doll.

Filming a scene from *Mad Love*. Drew starred opposite Chris O'Donnell as a bipolar teenager who flees from home on a road trip with the sudden object of her affections.

On the set of *Mad Love* with director Antonia Bird.

Drew with co-star and real-life love interest Luke Wilson in a scene from *Home Fries*. Drew's portrayal of a pregnant fast-food restaurant employee was complicated by her relationship with Wilson, which suffered tension-filled lows and passionate highs during the filming.

As Josie Gellar in *Never Been Kissed*, Drew played a reporter who goes undercover at a local high school to report on modern teenagers. The film was the fledgling effort of Drew's production company, Flower Films, and a box office hit.

In another scene from *Never Been Kissed*, Drew as Josie dances with her English teacher and romantic interest Sam Coulson (Michael Vartan).

Drew in costume on the set of *Charlie's Angels*, the film that established her as a savvy and powerful Hollywood force. The big screen adaptation of the popular television series scored at the box office.

An advertisement in *The Hollywood Reporter* heralds the box office success of *Charlie's Angels.*

Recent photo of John Drew Barrymore and his daughter Drew, hiking in the Santa Monica Mountains. Photo courtesy of Michael Green.

Barrymorebelia

Once you start loving any of the Barrymores you find that, like jungle fever or lumbago, "it" comes back on you every now and then.

—ELSIE JANIS

LONG BEFORE America's affair with the Barrymores began, theatergoers loved the Drew family: handsome John Senior, called the best Irish comedian of his time; Louisa Lane Drew, versatile actress who managed the Arch Street Theatre in Philadelphia for thirty years; beautiful and witty Georgie Drew Barrymore, who died well before her time; and John Drew Jr., who was at one time the most famous thespian in the United States, "the first gentleman of the American stage." One can still buy autographs of the members of the Drew family as well as playbills, signed checks, postcards, photographs, and cabinet cards depicting them and their performances. Collectors particularly enjoy finding notices of performances that included more than one Drew in their lineup, and playbills and advertisements from the Arch Street Theatre in Philadelphia are particularly choice pieces of theatrical history.

Sidney White Drew, Louisa Lane Drew's adopted son, was so popular that he and his wife, Gladys Rankin, were described and lampooned in Christopher Morley's book, *The Haunted Bookshop* in 1919. The delight that Morley's characters feel at watching one of the Drews' marital comedies needs little explanation to be appreciated by his audience, most of whom would have enjoyed the experience themselves on numerous occasions. "Then the organ began to play 'O How I Hate to Get Up in the Morning' and the ever-delightful Mr. and Mrs. Drew appeared on the screen in one of their domestic comedies," Morley's narrator notes in a chapter called "Aubrey Goes to the Movies." "Lovers of the movies may well date a new screen era from the day those whimsical pantomimers set their wholesome and humane talent at the service of the arc light and the lens," he observes. Morley's characters try to add even more delight to the performance "by watching Sidney Drew's face through the magnifying lenses. They were disappointed in the result, however, as the pictures, when so enlarged, revealed all the cracks on the film. Mr. Drew's nose, the most amusing feature known to the movies, lost its quaintness when so augmented.... 'Why!' cried Titania, 'it makes his lovely nose look like the map of Florida.'" Everyone in America knew that nose.

THOUSANDS OF PHOTOGRAPHS of handsome Maurice Barrymore were sold during Barry's days as a matinee idol, but few remain today. The name, however, still means good entertainment—and excitement. The Theater Alliance of Greater Philadelphia offers "The Barrymore Awards," in honor of "one of the most distinguished American theatrical families," and thus the connection the Barrymores forged with Philadelphia through their relationship to the Drew family still exists today. The TexasEscapes.com website, devoted to travel, tourism, and "romancing the legend that is Texas," keeps alive the tale of Maurice's famous shootout in Marshall, Texas:

> Marshall was indirectly responsible for launching the Barrymore Dynasty. Maurice Barrymore was a relatively unknown actor when he passed through Marshall with an acting troupe. At a tavern near the railroad station, Barrymore was dining with a male friend and the friend's female companion, when a bartender insulted the woman. In the fracas that followed, the friend was killed and Barrymore wounded. His appearance at the trial brought him national attention....Perhaps more than he would have gotten as an actor.

A community website for Fort Lee, New Jersey, offers information about a 1901 benefit in Buckeister's Park to raise money for the land on Washington Avenue, where a fire house and community hall were eventually built. Maurice Barrymore and John Drew apparently performed that evening, and some note this benefit as one of Jack Barrymore's very early performances.

The fascination with the Barrymores has not dwindled in Fort Lee since that long-ago performance. In 2001, residents tried to save a house that had supposedly been inhabited from the late 1800s until 1905 by Maurice and Jack. Hopes of converting the dilapidated nineteenth-century Victorian home into a museum of film history died with the building's demolition in 2001.

John Axe, author, editor, artist, and collector, explained part of the appeal of the Barrymore family. "I have been interested in movies and movie stars all my life," he wrote. "Naturally I've known all about the Barrymores since I can remember anything....Their lives were always fascinating, as none of them were your regular 'types.'"

In 1990 Axe designed a sheet of Maurice Barrymore paper dolls to enhance the theme of that year's national convention of doll collectors, which was "The Columbian Exhibition Revisited." He worked from available photographs to recreate costumes Barrymore wore in his most famous roles, and one doll even depicts the former British amateur boxing champion bare-chested with his hands raised. (Axe's choice was particularly appropriate since Maurice Barrymore attended the Columbia Exhibition and even purchased a pair of tame skunks from an animal handler he met there.)

THE BARRYMORES ARE NOW a part of our culture, through language—written, spoken and preserved on record and film—and through their presence at so many of the important events of our past.

According to biographer James Kotsilibas-Davis, the name Barrymore was applied to a number of people who excelled, performed, or went over the top.

> The name "Barrymore" stood as a synonym for acting. Mahatma Ghandi was called "the Lionel Barrymore of the talking newspapers." Franklin Delano Roosevelt was "a newsreel Barrymore." Every leading man from Ian Keith to Adolphe Menjou was chided at some point in his career for imitating Jack's "Barrymore manner." Douglas Fairbanks Jr., when he gave a good performance, was called the "Boy Barrymore." Richard Dix was praised for "out-Barrymoreing Barrymore." *Time* magazine coined a word when it noted that Ethel on stage lowered her eyebrows and leered "Barrymorishingly."

According to John Kobler, another Barrymore biographer, the name was also used to denote a long family acting tradition—the Adler acting family was referred to as "the Jewish Barrymores."

The Barrymores were innovative, and they added phrases and inventions to performing and to American culture in general. Maurice Barrymore is said to be the first actor who was tied to a railroad track in a play, a bit of action that would afterward become a theatrical convention, eventually trickling down to cartoons and comedy shorts. While playing in *Under the Gaslight* with the Daly company, Maurice was supposed to be rescued from the dire (and at that time innovative) situation, but the motor that was supposed to move the locomotive ominously toward the actor refused to work. Maurice lay on the tracks, calling out six times the cue for the train, but to no avail.

Jack designed a type of shirt collar that was long and pointed, and it became known as "the Barrymore collar." Jack also credited himself with inventing what he called "idiot boards," chalkboards containing his lines in case he should forget them. (He was one of the few actors who could act and read at the same time, he quipped.) Vincent Sherman noted that Jack was quite skillful at using his blackboards. "A sidelong glance or turnaway that seemed natural would allow him to focus on his next line," wrote Sherman, who worked with Jack in *Counselor at Law.* These boards evolved into cue cards, and the stigma of using

Like Ethel, Lionel Barrymore worked until his health would no longer permit it. So doing, he inadvertently broke new ground for disabled actors. Parts were specially written to accommodate the elder Barrymore brother, who was confined to a wheelchair at the end of his long career.

them disappeared as the fast pace of live television demanded them. Today they are commonplace.

Maurice Costello gave Lionel credit for coining the phrase "galloping tintypes" to describe the early flickering films shown in nickelodeons. Lionel also described how as a young director in the new sound medium he had attached a microphone to a broomstick, inventing the first boom mic so that his actors could move about the stage as they spoke their lines. Significantly, Lionel was the first disabled actor who had special roles created for him so that he could continue to perform after he was confined to a wheelchair because of arthritis and a hip injury that never healed.

Lines from Barrymore performances made their way into our culture as catch phrases. Ethel's trademark

"That's all there is, there isn't anymore" was a line she contributed to the stage play *Sunday*, because she felt one of her exits was too abrupt. According to Barrymore biographer Margot Peters, all Ethel Barrymore imitators used the famous line thereafter. Leonard Maltin points out in his foreword that he was enamored of Jack's line from *Twentieth Century*, "I close the iron door on you!"

Jack Barrymore seems to have been the family member who most intrigued the public. His life and work were of great interest to Americans. He was often front page news. He was in San Francisco during the great earthquake of 1906, and he claimed that his reputation for odd behavior was enhanced when Diamond Jim Brady saw him wandering about the ruins of the city in his evening clothes. What Jack felt like doing, he did. He climbed

Mont Blanc, though he had no experience scaling heights at all. (He was issued a certificate that named him the sixty-first person to reach the top of the formidable mountain.) Arthur Lennig, film historian and biographer of such film personalities as Erich von Stroheim and Bela Lugosi, has been a fan of Barrymore's work for many years. He writes that Jack "had an overwhelming screen presence that radiated intelligence, personality, and panache." And the roles he chose were those of "flamboyant characters with ironic twists." Barrymore was often accused of simply acting like himself on screen, which added to his reputation and drew the public; they knew he would offer a good show no matter the venue. Albert Einstein said, "Several mathematicians understand my theories, but of all persons it is an actor, John Barrymore, who discusses them most intelligently." Director and actor Vincent Sherman recalls Jack as "a truly cultured man, well read, with a knowledge of music and painting. Yet," adds Sherman, "there was something simple and down to earth about him." The first time Sherman read for a part Jack Barrymore asked him if he'd ever seen himself on film. "I want to warn you," he told the neophyte, "if you've never seen yourself on the screen, it'll be a shock to you, the way you look and sound. The first time I saw myself I went outside and puked." To Greta Garbo, he was "one of the very few who had that divine madness without which a great artist cannot work or live." His personality was intriguing to the ordinary American filmgoer as well as to the famous and celebrated. The fact that he attracts fans and collectors sixty years after his death is testimony to America's continuing fascination with the man and the legend.

According to Ruth Townsend, an avid fan and a collector who owns many personal items of the late actor, "in my opinion, John Barrymore was the greatest actor of the century....Even in roles where he was said to be mediocre, he was still great." And he was such a handsome rascal that people took an interest in his life as well as his work. On June 7, 1942, twenty-year-old war bride Martha Toomer wrote to her husband, Sheldon, "So the great profile is dead. With that many wives I'd be dead too!" Sheldon's answer did not survive, but Gene Fowler's biography on Barrymore, *Good Night, Sweet Prince*, "received the greatest acclaim from Yanks overseas of any work

printed during World War II," writes Fowler's son Will. The book was Fowler's masterpiece, and he recognized its success when his publisher, hampered by the wartime paper shortage, purchased another publishing concern so he could make use of their government allotment of paper to reprint. The book was also translated into Braille.

In 1997, Christopher Plummer toured in William Luce's play *Barrymore*. Ruth Townsend, who attended several performances, described the show. "It was a two-man show," she said, "although the second character was just an off-stage voice and never seen. Plummer comes out wheeling a portable bar and goes into a monologue of reminiscences. He is perfect. He bears a strong resemblance to Barrymore and his manner of speaking is as elegant as John's was. Of course, there are some bawdy tales and cursing—but he is after all BARRYMORE. He tells many of the famous Barrymore stories, some apocryphal, some true....Even people who have never heard of Barrymore find the play highly amusing." Townsend expresses sentiments common to all Jack Barrymore fans today. "I feel that I 'know' him in a way," she writes, "as I have spent so much time reading, researching, and collecting things by and about him. I wish I could have seen him on the stage in his heyday."

People still love the Barrymores, and items they have owned as well as memorabilia about them is treasured, sought after, bartered, and hoarded. And now there is Drew, who promises to become an industry herself. Every online auction site has Drew Barrymore collectibles: signed photos, publicity stills, press kits, movie shots, autographed posters, E.T. pocketbooks, E.T. children's books, and anything else she has touched or been associated with. Drew's Aunt Ethel was made into a collectible porcelain figurine, signed and numbered, meant to be displayed on a shelf or kept in the box to rise in value. Drew, representing modern, energetic womanhood, was, appropriately, made into an action figure in a bubble pack like all the other superheroes and movie dolls.

A desire to know the Royal Family of Hollywood drives collectors of Barrymorebelia. By purchasing items that belonged to a Barrymore, seeing movies that included one or more of them, reading books by and about them, and encouraging the heirs to success whenever possible, Americans pay their homage to their royal family.

The Barrymore family provided too much good material for well-known playwrights George S. Kaufman and Edna Ferber to pass up. Their *Royal Family* was not officially based on the Barrymores, but the parody was real enough to bother Ethel; Jack, on the other hand, liked the character supposedly based on him.

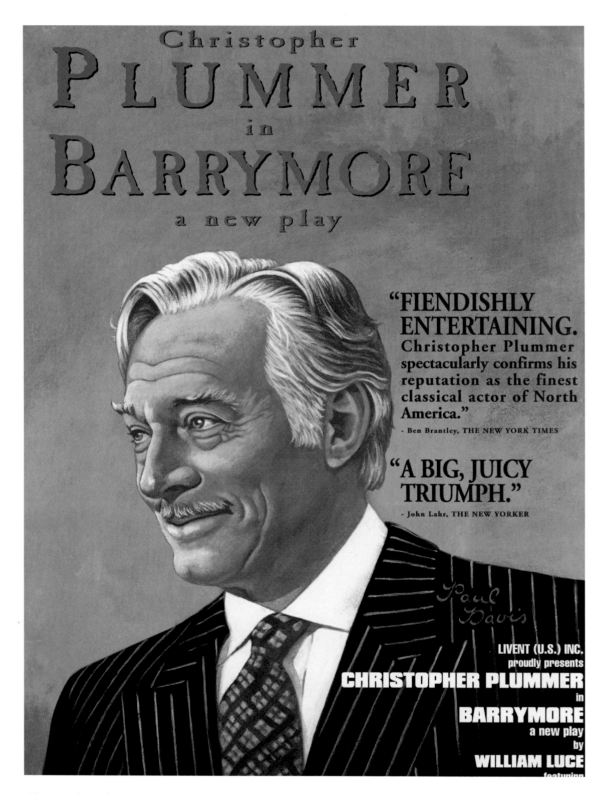

Christopher Plummer won positive reviews (and a Tony) as John Barrymore in the two-act play by William Luce.

Beautiful Dolores Costello on the cover of an early issue of *Motion Picture.* Websites today honor the "Goddess of the Silent Screen."

Maurice Costello

Maurice Costello postcards. One features a note asking the recipient to vote for Costello for the *Ladies' World* Moving Picture Contest.

POST CARD

THIS SIDE MAY BE USED FOR CORRESPONDENCE

THIS SIDE FOR ADDRESS ONLY

Dear Friend:
A mutual friend of ours wants me to win The Ladies' World Moving Picture Contest, the biggest one ever run. Will you vote for me?

Maurice Costello

You can vote. Full particulars and COUPON WORTH TEN VOTES in the current Ladies' World—now on the newsstands. Read how to get ten beautiful post cards and a large portrait of your favorite actor.
GET YOUR LADIES' WORLD TODAY.

Miss E. Irene Scroggs
1121 Claremont St.
City.

The Great Barrymores were honored by a U.S. postage stamp issued in 1982.

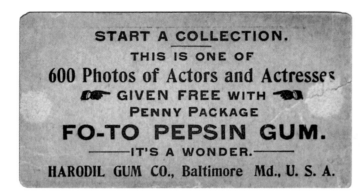

This Ethel Barrymore card was one of 600 Photos of Actors and Actresses given free with Penny Package Fo-to Pepsin Gum.

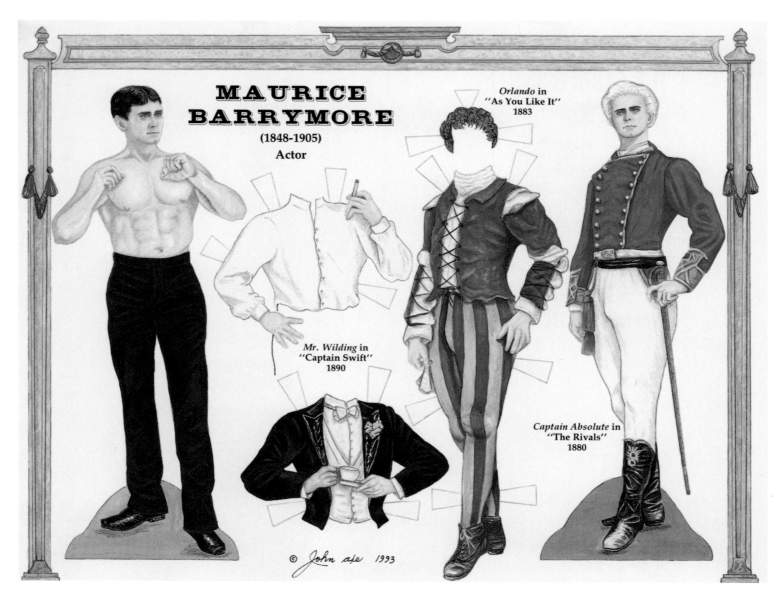

Maurice Barrymore paper dolls designed by John Axe feature costumes from the actor's most famous roles. Courtesy of John Axe.

Sheet music for the title song from Dolores Costello's *Glad Rag Doll* (1929).

Barrymore movie posters: *Grand Hotel* (1932) starring Jack and Lionel; *Little Lord Fauntleroy* (1936), starring Dolores; and *Te Esperaré en el Infierno* (1960), starring John Drew Barrymore. Lobby cards are one of the film buffs' favorite collectibles.

Barrymore actors and spokespersons: John for Kuppenheimer suits, Ethel for Heatherbloom slips, and Diana for Lux Soap.

RESIDENCE OF MR. AND MRS. JOHN BARRYMORE (DOLORES COSTELLO), BEVERLY HILLS

This illustration of John Barrymore and Dolores Costello's Beverly Hills home is one of eighteen featured in a "Homes of California Movie Stars" postcard from the 1940s.

Old Red Bank   Lionel Barrymore

An etching of "Old Red Bank" by Lionel Barrymore. In the 1960s sets of prints were produced and marketed as premiums and free gifts from banks and business.

A clipping from the Sunday funnies shows Jack in his
Circus of the Stars costume.

A Mr. Hyde puzzle
with its own film can.

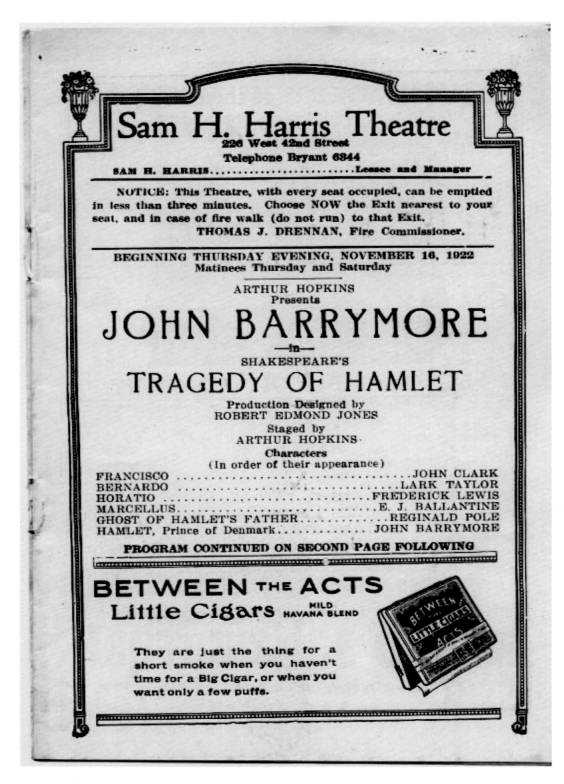

An advertisement for Jack's most famous role—that of Hamlet.

Matchbook advertising Jack's last play, *My Dear Children*.

Director Vincent Sherman still occasionally listens to Barrymore's rich voice on vinyl. "I treasure my memory of him," says Sherman.

Marie Dressler and Lionel Barrymore poster from *Christopher Bean.*

The diary and ship's log that Dolores Costello and Jack Barrymore kept on their honeymoon and dedicated to her mother, Mae Costello.

Drew Barrymore in a publicity shot with a striped cat, taken around ten years of age, about the time she was playing in *Cat's Eye* (1985), written by Stephen King.

Drew Barrymore, actress, businesswoman, and founder of Flower Films, 2001.

Filmographies

Diana Blanche Blyth Barrymore
(1921-1960)

AS ACTRESS

1941   *Manpower* (uncredited)
1942   *Between Us Girls*
      Eagle Squadron
      Nightmare
1943   *Fired Wife*
      Frontier Badmen
1944   *Adventures of Mark Twain, The*
      Hollywood Canteen (uncredited)
      Ladies Courageous, aka *Fury in the Sky*
1950   *D.O.A.* (uncredited)
1951   *Mob, The*

AS WRITER

1958   *Too Much, Too Soon* (book, with Cameron Shipp)

Doris Rankin Barrymore
(1880-1946)

AS ACTRESS

1920   *Copperhead, The*
      Devil's Garden, The
1921   *Great Adventure, The*
      Jim the Penman
1925   *Lena Rivers*
1930   *Her Unborn Child*
      Love at First Sight
1931   *Night Angel*
1936   *Come Closer, Folks* (uncredited)
1937   *Fit for a King* (uncredited)

      Hoosier Schoolboy, aka *Forgotten Hero*
1938   *Saleslady*
      You Can't Take It with You (uncredited)
1939   *Society Smugglers*
      When Tomorrow Comes (uncredited)

Drew Barrymore
(1975-)

AS ACTRESS

1978   *Suddenly, Love* (TV)
1980   *Altered States*
      Bogie (TV)
1982   *E.T. the Extra-Terrestrial*, aka *E.T.*
1984   *Firestarter*
      Irreconcilable Differences
1985   *Cat's Eye*, aka *Stephen King's Cat's Eye*
1986   *Babes in Toyland* (TV)
1987   *Conspiracy of Love* (TV)
1989   *Far from Home*
      See You in the Morning
1991   *Motorama*
1992   *Guncrazy*
      No Place to Hide
      Poison Ivy
      Sketch Artist (TV)
      Waxwork II: Lost in Time, aka *Lost in Time*, aka *Space Shift: Waxwork II*
1993   *Amy Fisher Story, The*, aka *Beyond Control* (TV)
      Doppelganger, aka *Doppelganger:*

      The Evil Within
      Wayne's World 2
1994   *Bad Girls*
      Inside the Goldmine
1995   *Batman Forever*, aka *Forever*
      Boys on the Side
      Mad Love
1996   *Everyone Says I Love You*
      Like a Lady
      Making of E.T. The Extra-Terrestrial, The
      Scream
1997   *Best Men*
      Wishful Thinking
1998   *Ever After*
      Home Fries
      Wedding Singer, The
1999   *Never Been Kissed*
      Olive, the Other Reindeer (TV)
2000   *Charlie's Angels*
      Skipped Parts
      So Love Returns
      Titan A.E., aka *Titan: After Earth*
2001   *Barbarella*
      Donnie Darko
      Duplex, The
      Riding in the Car with Boys

AS PRODUCER

1999   *Never Been Kissed*
      Olive, the Other Reindeer (TV)
2000   *Charlie's Angels*
      So Love Returns
2001   *Barbarella*
      Donnie Darko
      Duplex, The

Ethel Barrymore
(1879-1959)

AS ACTRESS

1914	*Nightingale, The*
1915	*Final Judgement, The*
1916	*Awakening of Helena Ritchie, The*
	Kiss of Hate, The
1917	*American Widow, An*
	Call of Her People, The
	Eternal Mother, The
	Life's Whirlpool
	Lifted Veil, The
	Greatest Power, The, aka *Her Greatest Power*
	National Red Cross Pageant (with Jack Barrymore and Lionel Barrymore)
	White Raven, The
1918	*Our Mrs. McChesney*
1919	*Divorcee, The*
1932	*Rasputin and the Empress* (with Jack Barrymore and Lionel Barrymore)
1933	*All at Sea*
1944	*None But the Lonely Heart*
1946	*Spiral Staircase, The*
1947	*Farmer's Daughter, The*
	Moss Rose
	Paradine Case, The
1948	*Moonrise*
	Night Song
	Portrait of Jennie
1949	*Great Sinner, The*
	Pinky
	Red Danube, The
	That Midnight Kiss
1951	*It's a Big Country*
	Kind Lady
	Secret of Convict Lake, The
1952	*Deadline*
	Just for You
1953	*Main Street to Broadway* (with Lionel Barrymore)
	Story of Three Loves, The, aka *Equilibrium,* aka *Three Stories of Love*
1954	*Young at Heart*
1957	*Johnny Trouble*

Irene Fenwick Barrymore
(1887-1936)

AS ACTRESS

1915	*Child of Destiny, The*
	Commuters, The
	Green Cloak, The
	Sentimental Lady
	Spendthrift, The
	Woman Next Door, The
1916	*Coney Island Princess, A*
1917	*Girl Like That, A*
	Sin Woman, The

John Blyth Barrymore
(1954-)

AS ACTOR

1976	*Baby Blue Marine*
1978	*Feedback*
	One Man Jury, aka *Dead on Arrival*
1979	*Nocturna,* aka *Granddaughter of Dracula*
1981	*Americana*
	Full Moon High
	Smokey Bites the Dust
1982	*Trick or Treats*
1984	*Hard to Hold*
1990	*Bonfire of the Vanities, The* (uncredited)
	Crazy People
	Cry Baby
	Rich Girl
	Solar Crisis (as John Barrymore)
1991	*Indian Runner, The* (uncredited)
	Love Crimes
	Ted and Venus
1992	*Landslide*
1993	*House in the Hills, A*
	Lucky ducks
1994	*Inner Sanctum II*
	Mind Twister
	Twogether
1996	*Last of the Breed*
	Masseuse, aka *American Masseuse*
1997	*Hybrid*

John Drew Barrymore
(1932-)

AS ACTOR

1950	*High Lonesome* (as John Barrymore Jr.)
	Sundowners, The (as John Barrymore Jr.)
1951	*Big Night, The* (as John Barrymore Jr.)
	Quebec (as John Barrymore Jr.)
1952	*Thunderbirds* (as John Barrymore Jr.)
1956	*While the City Sleeps* (as John Barrymore Jr.)
1957	*Shadow on the Window* (as John Barrymore Jr.)
1958	*High School Confidential!,* aka *Young Hellions* (USA: reissue title)
	Never Love a Stranger
1959	*Boatmen, The*
	Cossacks, The
	Night of the Quarter Moon, aka *Flesh and Flame*
1960	*Nuits de Raspoutine, Les,* aka *Giant Monster,* aka *Night They Killed Rasputin, The,* aka *Nights of Rasputin*
	Ti aspetteró all'inferno
1961	*Donna dei faraoni, La,* aka *Pharoah's Woman, The*
1962	*Col ferro e col fuoco,* aka *Daggers of Blood,* aka *Invasion 1700, With Fire and Sword*
	Conquistatore di Corinto, Il, aka *Centurion, The,* aka *Conqueror of Corinth*
	Pontius Pilate
	Guerra di Troia, La, aka *Trojan Horse, The,* aka *Trojan War, The,* aka *Wooden Horse of Troy, The*
	Roma contro roma, aka *Night Star: Goddess of Electra,* aka *War of the Zombies*
1963	*Diavoli di spartivento, I,* aka *Curse of the Haunted Forest,* aka *Devils of Spartivento, The,* aka *Fighting Legions, The,* aka *Weapons of Vengeance*
	Keeler Affair, The, aka *Christine*

1964 *Keeler Affair, The*
Delitto allo specchio, aka *Death on the Fourposter,* aka *Sexy Party*
1965 *Crimine a due,* aka *Casa sulla fungaia, La*
1974 *Clones, The,* aka *Cloning of Dr. Appleby, The,* aka *Cloning, The,* aka *Dead Man Running,* aka *Mindsweepers, The* (as John Barrymore Jr.)

John Sidney Blyth Barrymore
(1882-1942)

AS ACTOR

1912 *Dream of a Motion Picture Director* (uncredited)
Prize Package, A (uncredited)
Widow Casey's Return, The
1913 *One on Romance* (uncredited)
1914 *American Citizen, An*
Man from Mexico, The
1915 *Are You a Mason?*
Dictator, The
Incorrigible Dukane, The
1916 *Lost Bridegroom, The,* aka *His Lost Self*
Nearly a King
Red Widow, The
1917 *National Red Cross Pageant* (with Lionel Barrymore and Ethel Barrymore)
Raffles, the Amateur Cracksman, aka *Raffles*
1918 *On the Quiet*
1919 *Here Comes the Bride*
Test of Honor, The
1920 *Dr. Jekyll and Mr. Hyde*
1921 *Lotus Eater, The*
1922 *Sherlock Holmes*
1924 *Beau Brummel*
1926 *Don Juan*
Sea Beast, The (with Dolores Costello)
1927 *Beloved Rogue, The*
When a Man Loves (with Dolores Costello)
1928 *Tempest*
1929 *Eternal Love*
Show of Shows, The (with Dolores Costello)
1930 *General Crack*
Man from Blankley's, The
Moby Dick
1931 *Mad Genius, The*
Svengali
1932 *Arséne Lupin* (with Lionel Barrymore)
Bill of Divorcement, A
Grand Hotel (with Lionel Barrymore)
Rasputin and the Empress (with Lionel Barrymore and Ethel Barrymore)
State's Attorney
1933 *Counsellor at Law*
Dinner at Eight (with Lionel Barrymore)
Hamlet—Act I: Scene V
Night Flight (with Lionel Barrymore)
Reunion in Vienna
Topaze
1934 *Long Lost Father*
Twentieth Century
1936 *Romeo and Juliet*
1937 *Bulldog Drummond Comes Back*
Bulldog Drummond's Revenge
Maytime
Night Club Scandal
True Confession
1938 *Bulldog Drummond's Peril*
Hold That Co-ed
Marie Antoinette
Romance in the Dark
Spawn of the North
1939 *Great Man Votes, The*
Midnight
1940 *Great Profile, The*
Invisible Woman, The
1941 *Playmates*
Unusual Occupations, uncredited
World Premiere

Katherine Corri Harris Barrymore
(1893-1927)

AS ACTRESS

1916 *Lost Bridegroom, The* (as Katherine Harris Barrymore)
Nearly a King (as Katherine Harris)
1918 *House of Mirth, The* (as Katherine Harris Barrymore)

Lionel Herbert (Blyth) Barrymore
(1878-1954)

AS ACTOR

1908 *Paris Hat, The*
1911 *Battle, The*
Fighting Blood
Miser's Heart, The
1912 *Brutality*
Burglar's Dilemma, The
Chief's Blanket, The
Cry for Help, A
Friends
God Within, The
Gold and Glitter
Heredity
Home Folks
Informer, The
Musketeers of Pig Alley, The
My Baby
My Hero
New York Hat, The
One She Loved, The
Painted Lady, The
So Near, Yet So Far
Unseen Enemy, An (uncredited)
1913 *Adventure in the Autumn Woods, An*
All for Science
Almost a Wild Man
Chance Deception, A
Crook and the Girl, The
Death's Marathon
Enemy's Baby, The
Fate
Gamble with Death, A
Girl's Stratagem, A
House of Darkness, The
House of Discord, The
I Was Meant for You
In Diplomatic Circles
Indian's Loyalty, An
Just Gold
Lady and the Mouse, The
Little Tease, The

Massacre, The

Mirror, The   1917

Misunderstood Boy, A

Near to Earth

Oil and Water

Perfidy of Mary, The

Ranchero's Revenge, The

Red Hicks Defies the World   1920

Sheriff's Baby, The

So Runs the Way

Stolen Treaty, The

Strong Man's Burden, The   1921

Switch Tower, The

Telephone Girl and the Lady, The   1922

Tender Hearted Boy, The

Three Friends   1923

Timely Interception, A

Under the Shadow of the Law

Unwelcome Guest, The   1924

Wanderer, The

Well, The

Work Habit, The

Wrong Bottle, The

Yaqui Cur, The   1925

1914 Battle at Elderbush Gulch, The,
aka Battle of Elderbush Gulch,
The

Brute Force, aka In Prehistoric
Days, aka Primitive Man; Wars of
the Primal Tribes

Classmates

Exploits of Elaine, The   1926

Judith of Bethulia

Men and Women

Power of the Press, The

Seats of the Mighty, The

Span of Life, The

Strongheart

Under the Gaslight   1927

Woman in Black, The

1915 Curious Conduct of Judge Legarde,
The, aka Valley of Night, The

Dora Thorne

Flaming Sword, The

Modern Magdalen, A

Romance of Elaine, The

Wildfire

Yellow Streak, A

1916 Brand of Cowardice, The

Dorian's Divorce

Quitter, The   1929

Upheaval, The

End of the Tour, The

His Father's Son

Millionaire's Double, The

National Red Cross Pageant (with
Jack Barrymore and Ethel
Barrymore)

Copperhead, The

Devil's Garden, The

Master Mind, The, aka Sinners
Three

Great Adventure, The

Jim the Penman

Boomerang Bill

Face in the Fog, The

Enemies of Women

Eternal City, The

Unseeing Eyes

America

Decameron Nights

I Am the Man

Meddling Women

Wedding Women

Children of the Whirlwind

Fifty-Fifty

Frau mit dem schlechten Ruf, Die

Girl Who Wouldn't Work, The

Man of Iron, A, aka Iron Man,
The

Splendid Road, The

Wrongdoers, The

Barrier, The

Bells, The

Brooding Eyes

Lucky Lady, The

Paris at Midnight

Temptress, The

Wife Tamers

Body and Soul

Show, The

Thirteenth Hour, The

Women Love Diamonds

Alias Jimmy Valentine

Drums of Love, aka Sentimental
Tommy

Lion and the Mouse, The

River Woman, The

Road House

Sadie Thompson

West of Zanzibar

Hollywood Revue of 1929, The,

aka Hollywood Revue, The

Mysterious Island, The

1930 Free and Easy

1931 Christmas Party, The, aka
Christmas Story, A (uncredited)

Free Soul, A

Guilty Hands

Mata Hari

Movie Album, The

Yellow Ticket, The

1932 Arséne Lupin (with Jack
Barrymore)

Broken Lullaby

Grand Hotel (with Jack
Barrymore)

Rasputin and the Empress (with
Jack Barrymore and Ethel
Barrymore)

Washington Masquerade

1933 Berkeley Square

Christopher Bean, aka Her
Sweetheart, Christopher Bean

Dinner at Eight (with Jack
Barrymore)

Looking Forward, aka New Deal,
The

Night Flight (with Jack
Barrymore)

One Man's Journey

Should Ladies Behave

Stranger's Return, The

Sweepings

1934 Carolina

Ciudad de cartón, La, aka
Cardboard City, aka Hollywood,
ciudad de cartón

Girl from Missouri, The, aka Born
to Be Kissed (USA)

This Side of Heaven

Treasure Island

1935 Ah, Wilderness!

David Copperfield

Little Colonel, The

Mark of the Vampire, aka
Vampires of Prague

Public Hero #1

Return of Peter Grimm, The

1936 Devil-Doll, The, aka Witch of
Timbuctoo, The

Gorgeous Hussy, The

Road to Glory, The

	Voice of Bugle Ann, The
1937	*Camille*
	Captains Courageous
	Family affair, A, aka *Skidding,* aka *Stand Accused*
	Navy Blue and Gold
	Saratoga
1938	*Test Pilot*
	Yank at Oxford, A
	You Can't Take It with You
	Young Dr. Kildare
1939	*Calling Dr. Kildare*
	Let Freedom Ring
	On Borrowed Time
	Secret of Dr. Kildare, The
1940	*Dr. Kildare Goes Home*
	Dr. Kildare's Crisis
	Dr. Kildare's Strange Case
1941	*Bad Man, The,* aka *Two-Gun Cupid*
	Dr. Kildare's Victory
	Dr. Kildare's Wedding Day
	Lady Be Good
	People vs. Dr. Kildare, The
	Penalty, The
1942	*Calling Dr. Gillespie*
	Dr. Gillespie's New Assistant
	Tennessee Johnson
1943	*Dr. Gillespie's Criminal Case*
	Guy Named Joe, A
	Last Will and Testament of Tom Smith, The, aka *War Information Film No. 76*
	Some of the Best
	Thousands Cheer (uncredited)
1944	*Between Two Women*
	Dragon Seed (uncredited)
	Since You Went Away
	Three Men in White
1945	*Valley of Decision, The*
1946	*Duel in the Sun*
	It's a Wonderful Life
	Secret Heart, The
	Three Wise Fools
1947	*Dark Delusion*
1948	*Key Largo*
1949	*Down to the Sea in Ships*
	Malaya, aka *Alien Orders*
1950	*Metro-Goldwyn-Mayer Story, The*
	Right Cross
	Screen Actors (uncredited)

1951	*Bannerline*
	Lone Star
1953	*Main Street to Broadway* (with Ethel Barrymore)
1955	*Film Fun*

AS DIRECTOR

1913	*Chocolate Dynamite*
	His Secret
	Just Boys
	No Place for Father
	Where's the Baby?
1917	*Life's Whirlpool*
1929	*Confession*
	His Glorious Night, aka *Breath of Scandal*
	Madame X
	Unholy Night, The, aka *Green Ghost, The*
1930	*Rogue Song, The*
1931	*Guilty Hands* (uncredited)
	Ten Cents a Dance

AS WRITER

1912	*Burglar's Dilemma, The*
1913	*Tender Hearted Boy, The*
	Vengeance of Galora, The
1917	*Life's Whirlpool* (scenario)

AS COMPOSER

| 1929 | *His Glorious Night,* aka *Breath of Scandal* |
| 1941 | *Dr. Kildare's Wedding Day* |

Dolores Costello
(1903-1979)

AS ACTRESS

1909	*Midsummer Night's Dream, A* (with Maurice Costello and Helene Costello)
1910	*Telephone, The*
1911	*Child Crusoes, The* (with Helene Costello)
	Geranium, A (with Maurice Costello and Helene Costello)
	His Sister's Children (with Maurice Costello and Helene Costello)

	Meeting of the Ways, The
1912	*Captain Jenks' Dilemma* (with Helene Costello)
	Ida's Christmas
	Juvenile Love Affair, A
	Lulu's Doctor (with Maurice Costello with Helene Costello*
	Money King, The (with Maurice Costello)
	Toymaker, The with Helene Costello)
	Troublesome Step-Daughters, The (with Helene Costello)
1913	*Fellow Voyagers* (with Maurice Costello and Helene Costello)
	Hindoo Charm, The (with Maurice Costello and Helene Costello)
1914	*How Cissy Made Good* (with Helene Costello)
1915	*Evil Men Do, The* (with Maurice Costello and Helene Costello)
1923	*Glimpses of the Moon, The* (with Maurice Costello)
	Lawful Larceny
1925	*Bobbed Hair* (with Helene Costello)
	Greater Than a Crown
1926	*Bride of the Storm*
	Little Irish Girl, The
	Mannequin
	Third Degree, The
	Sea Beast, The
1927	*College Widow, The*
	Heart of Maryland, The (with Helene Costello)
	Million Bid, A
	Old San Francisco
	When a Man Loves
1928	*Glorious Betsy*
	Tenderloin
1929	*Glad Rag Doll*
	Hearts in Exile
	Madonna of Avenue, A
	Noah's Ark
	Redeeming Sin, The
	Show of Shows, The (with Helene Costello)
1930	*Second Choice*
1931	*Expensive Women*
1936	*Little Lord Fauntleroy*

Yours for the Asking (as Dolores Costello Barrymore)

1938 *Beloved Brat*
Breaking the Ice

1939 *King of the Turf*
Outside These Walls
Whispering Enemies

1942 *Magnificent Ambersons, The*

1943 *This Is the Army*

Helene Costello
(1902-1957)

AS ACTRESS

1909 *Galley Slave, The,* aka *Les Miserables (Part I)* (with Maurice Costello)
Midsummer Night's Dream (with Dolores Costello and Maurice Costello)

1911 *Auld Lang Syne*
Captain Barnacle's Baby
Child Crusoes, The (with Dolores Costello)
Her Crowning Glory
His Sister's Children (with Dolores Costello and Maurice Costello)
Geranium, A (with Dolores Costello and Maurice Costello)
Old Doll, The

1912 *At Scrogginse's Corner* (as Helen Costello)
Black Sheep, The
Captain Barnacle's Messmate
Captain Jenks' Dilemma (with Dolores Costello)
Church Across the Way, The (as Helen Costello)
Cleopatra, aka *Helen Gardner in Cleopatra*
First Violin, The (with Maurice Costello)
Greatest Thing in the World, The
In the Garden Fair
Lulu's Doctor (with Dolores Costello and Maurice Costello)
Night Before Christmas, The (with Maurice Costello)
Rip Van Winkle

Toymaker, The (with Dolores Costello)
Troublesome Step-Daughters (with Dolores Costello)
Two Women and Two Men
Wanted...a Grandmother

1913 *Beau Brummel*
Christmas Story, A
Doctor's Secret, The
Fellow Voyagers (with Dolores Costello and Maurice Costello)
Fortune's Turn
Heartbroken Shep
Hindoo Charm, The (with Dolores Costello and Maurice Costello)
Matrimonial Manoeuvres (with Maurice Costello)
Mr. Bolter's Niece
Mystery of the Stolen Child (with Maurice Costello)
Other Woman, The
Tim Grogan's Foundling

1914 *Barrel Organ, The*
How Cissy Made Good (with Dolores Costello)
Memories That Haunt, The (as Helen Costello)
Some Steamer Scooping (with Maurice Costello)

1915 *Evil Men Do, The* (with Dolores Costello and Maurice Costello)
Living the Ban of Coventry

1925 *Bobbed Hair* (with Dolores Costello)
Man on the Box, The
Ranger of the Big Pines

1926 *Don Juan* (uncredited)
Honeymoon Express, The
Love Toy, The
Millionaires
Wet Paint
While London Sleeps

1927 *Broncho Twister, The*
Finger Prints
Fortune Hunter, The
Good Time Charley
Heart of Maryland, The (with Dolores Costello Barrymore)
Husbands for Rent
In Old Kentucky

1928 *Broken Barriers*
Burning Up Broadway
Circus Kid, The
Comrades
Lights of New York
Midnight Taxi, The
Phantom of the Turf

1929 *Fatal Warning, The*
Innocents of Paris
Show of Shows, The (with Dolores Costello Barrymore)
When Dreams Come True

1931 *Movie Album, The* (with Maurice Costello)

1935 Public Hero #1 (uncredited)

1936 *Riffraff*

Mae Altshuh Costello
(1882-1929)

AS ACTRESS

1911 *Her Crowning Glory* (as Mrs. Maurice Costello)

1915 *Women a Woman Loves*

1917 *Her Right to Live*
Money Mill, The

Maurice Costello
(1877-1950)

AS ACTOR

1905 *Adventures of Sherlock Holmes,* aka *Adventures of Sherlock Holmes; or, Held for Ransom*

1908 *Antony and Cleopatra*
Bride of Lammermoor, The
Dancer and the King: A Romantic Story of Spain, The, aka *Dancer and the King, The*
Ex-Convict No. 900
Julius Caesar
Kenilworth
King Lear (undetermined role)
Leah the Forsaken
Merchant of Venice, The (undetermined role)
Richard III, aka *Richard III: A Shakespearean Tragedy*
Ruy Blas

Salome

Slippery Jim's Repentance

Virginius

1909 *Duke's Jester or A Fool's Revenge,*
The

Galley Slave, The, aka *Les*
Miserables (Part I) (with Helene
Costello)

Gift of Youth, The

Les Misérables, aka *Jean Valjean*

Midsummer Night's Dream, A
(with Dolores Costello and
Helene Costello)

Plot That Failed, The

Power of the Press, The

Richelieu or The Conspiracy

Saul and David

Way of the Cross, The

1910 *Capital vs. Labor*

Conscience, aka *Baker Boy, The*

Convict No. 796

Elktra

Love of Chrysanthemum

Over the Garden Wall

Uncle Tom's Cabin

1911 *Battle Hymn of the Republic, The*

Captain Barnacle, Diplomat

Changing of Silas Warner, The

Dead Man's Honor, A

Geranium, A (with Dolores
Costello and Helene Costello)

Her Hero

His Mother

His Sister's Children (with
Dolores Costello and Helene
Costello)

His Wife's Secret

My Old Dutch

New Stenographer, The

Sacrifice, The

Society and the Man

Tale of Two Cities

Thumb Print, The

Wooing of Winnifred, The

1912 *Adventure of the Italian Model,*
The

Adventure of the Retired Army
Colonel, The

As You Like It

Aunty's Romance

Conscience, aka *Chamber of*

Horrors, The

Counsel for the Defense

Diamond Brooch, The

Dr. LaFleur's Theory

First Violin, The (with Helene
Costello)

Flirt of Heroine

For the Honor of the Family

Half a Hero

Jocular Winds of Fate, The

Law or the Lady, The

Lord Browning and Cinderella

Lulu's Doctor (with Dolores
Costello and Helene Costello)

Mistake in Spelling, A

Money King, The

Mrs. 'Enry 'Awkins

Nemesis!

Night Before Christmas, The
(with Helene Costello)

Old Kent Road, The

Old Silver Watch, The

On the Pupil of His Eye

Picture Idol, The

Spider's Web, The

Their Golden Anniversary

Two Battles, The

Vitagraph Romance, A

Wanted...a Grandmother (with
Helene Costello)

When Roses Wither

Winning Is Losing

1913 *Adventure of the Ambassador's*
Disappearance, The

Adventures of the Counterfeit Bills,
The

Cupid Versus Women's Rights

Delayed Proposals

Fellow Voyagers (with Dolores
Costello and Helene Costello)

Getting Up a Practice

Hindoo Charm, The (with
Dolores Costello and Helene
Costello)

Matrimonial Manoeuvres (with
Helene Costello)

Mr. Mintern's Misadventures

Mystery of the Stolen Child (with
Helene Costello)

On Their Wedding Eve

Princess of Bagdad, A

Taming of Betty, The

Way Out, The

What a Change of Clothes Did

1914 *Mill of Life, The*

Moonstone of Fez, The

Mr. Barnes of New York

Mysterious Lodger, The

Perplexed Bridegroom, The

Some Steamer Scooping (with
Helene Costello)

Woman in Black, The

1915 *Criminal, The*

Crown Prince's Double, The

Dawn of Understanding, The

Dorothy

Evil Men Do, The (with Dolores
Costello and Helene Costello)

Gods Redeem, The

Man Who Couldn't Beat God, The

Question of Right or Wrong, A

Rags and the Girl

Romance of a Handkerchief, The

Saints and Sinners

Tried for His Own Murder

1916 *Crimson Stain Mystery, The*

1919 *Cambric Mask*

Captain's Captain, The, aka
Cap'n Abe's Niece

Girl-Woman, The

Man Who Won, The

1920 *Deadline at Eleven*

Human Collateral

Tower of Jewels, The

1921 *Conceit*

1922 *Determination*

1923 *Fog Bound*

Glimpses of the Moon, The (with
Dolores Costello)

Man and Wife

None So Blind

1924 *Heart of Alaska*

Law and the Lady, The

Let Not Man Put Asunder

Love of Women

Roulette

Story Without a Name, The, aka
Without Warning

Virtuous Liars

Week End Husbands

1925 *Mad Marriage, The*

1926 *False Alarm, The*

	Last Alarm, The
	Wives of the Prophet, The
1927	*Camille*
	Johnny Get Your Hair Cut
	Shamrock and the Rose, The
	Spider Webs
	Wolves of the Air
1928	*Black Feather*
	Eagle of the Night
	Wagon Show, The
1931	*Movie Album, The* (with Helene Costello)
1936	*Hollywood Boulevard*
1939	*Andy Hardy Gets Spring Fever*
	Five Little Peppers and How They Grew (uncredited)
	Happily Buried (uncredited)
	It's a Wonderful World (uncredited)
	Mr. Smith Goes to Washington (uncredited)
	Roaring Twenties, The (uncredited)
	Rovin' Tumbleweeds
1940	*Little Bit of Heaven, A*
1941	*Here Comes Mr. Jordan* (uncredited)
	Lady from Louisiana, aka *Lady from New Orleans*
1942	*Reap the Wild Wind* (uncredited)
1943	*Du Barry Was a Lady* (uncredited)

AS DIRECTOR

1912	*Conscience,* aka *Chamber of Horrors, The*
1913	*Adventure of the Ambassador's Disappearance, The*
	Cupid Versus Women's Rights
	Extremities
	Fellow Voyagers
	Getting Up a Practice
	Hindoo Charm, The
	Matrimonial Manoeuvres
	Mystery of the Stolen Child
	On Their Wedding Eve
	What a Change of Clothes Did
1914	*Her Great Scoop*
	Moonstone of Fez, The
	Mr. Barnes of New York

	Mysterious Lodger, The
	Perplexed Bridgegroom, The
	Woman in Black, The
1915	*Evil Men Do, The*
	Man Who Couldn't Beat God, The

AS WRITER

1912	*Aunty's Romance*

Gladys Rankin Drew
(1874-1914)

AS WRITER

1913	*Late Mr. Jones, The* (as George Cameron)
	Sweet Deception
1914	*Million Bid, A* (as George Cameron) play
1915	*Thou Art the Man* (as George Cameron) story
1927	*Million Bid, A* (as George Cameron) play

Lucille McVey Drew
(1890-1925)

AS ACTRESS

1914	*Auntie's Portrait*
	Florida Enchantment, A (as Jane Morrow)
	Too Many Husbands (as Jane Morrow)
1915	*All for a Girl,* aka *All for the Love of a Girl*
	Fox Trot Finesse
	Is Christmas a Bore?
	Playing Dead
	Safe Investment, A
1916	*Duplicity*
1917	*As Other See Us*
	Close Resemblance, A
	Dentist, The
	Henry's Ancestors
	Her Anniversaries
	Her Economic Independence
	Her First Love
	Her Lesson
	His Curiosity
	His Deadly Calm

	His Double Life
	Hypochondriacs
	Lest We Forget
	One of the Finest
	Patriot, The
	Pest, The
	Rubbing It In
	Safety First
	Shadowing Henry
	Too Much Henry
	Twelve Good Hens and True
	Why they Left Home, aka *Why Henry Left Home*
1918	*After Henry*
	Before and After Taking
	Gas Logic
	His First Love
	Pay Day
	Special Today
	Youthful Affair, A
1919	*Amateur Liar, The*
	Bunkered
	Harold, the Last of the Saxons
	Once a Mason
	Romance and Rings
	Sisterly Scheme, A
	Squared
1920	*Charming Mrs. Chase, The*
	Emotional Miss Vaughn, The

AS WRITER

1915	*Playing Dead*
1917	*Close Resemblance, A*
	Her Anniversaries
	Her Lesson
	His Curiosity
	Lest We Forget
	Patriot, The
	Rubbing It In
	Safety First
	Shadowing Henry
	Too Much Henry
	Why They Left Home, aka *Why Henry Left Home*
1918	*After Henry*
	Before and After Taking
	Gas Logic
	His First Love
	Pay Day
	Special Today
	Youthful Affair, A

1919   Amateur Liar, The
        Bunkered
        Gay Old Dog, A
        Harold, the Last of the Saxons
        Once a Mason
        Romance and Rings
        Sisterly Scheme, A
        Squared
1920   Charming Mrs. Chase, The
        Emotional Miss Vaughn, The

AS DIRECTOR

1917   Close Resemblance, A
        Her Anniversaries
        Her Lesson
        His Curiosity
        Lest We Forget
        Patriot, The
        Rubbing It In
        Safety First
        Shadowing Henry
        Too Much Henry
        Why They Left Home, aka Why
        Henry Left Home
1918   After Henry
        Before and After Taking
        Gas Logic
        His First Love
        Pay Day
        Special Today
1919   Amateur Liar, The
        Bunkered
        Harold, the Last of the Saxons
        Once a Mason
        Sisterly Scheme, A
        Squared
1920   Charming Mrs. Chase, The
1921   Cousin Kate

Sidney Rankin Drew
(1892-1918)

AS ACTOR

1913   Game of Cards, A
        Glove, The
        His Tired Uncle
        Idler, The
        Internal Triangle, An
        Maria's Sacrifice
        Marrying Sue

        My Lady of Idleness
        Penalties of Reputation, The
        Snare of Fate, The
        Still Voice, The (as Sidney Drew
        Jr.)
        Tattoo Mark, The
        Unwritten Chapter, An
1914   Drudge, The
        Idler
        In the Latin Quarter
        Mr. Barnes of New York
1915   Elsa's Brother
        Island of Regeneration, The
        Janet of the Chorus
        O'Garry of the Royal Mounted
        Quality of Mercy, The
        Thou Art the Man
1916   Girl Philippa, The
        Hunted Woman, The
        Suspect, The
        Third Party, The
        Who Killed Joe Merrion?
1919   Belle of the Season, The

AS DIRECTOR

1915   Love's Way
        Thou Art the Man
        What's Ours?
1916   Daring of Diana, The
        Girl Philippa, The
        Hunted Woman, The
        Kennedy Square
        Suspect, The
        Vital Question, The
1917   Who's Your Neighbor?
1919   Belle of the Season, The

AS WRITER

1916   Suspect, The
1917   Who's Your Neighbor?
1919   Belle of the Season, The

Sidney White Drew
(1863-1919)

AS ACTOR

1911   Red Devils, The
        When Two Hearts Are Won
1914   Auntie's Portrait

        Florida Enchantment, A
        Goodness Gracious, aka Goodness
        Gracious; or Movies as They
        Shouldn't Be
        Horseshoe—For Luck
        Innocent But Awkward
        Jerry's Uncle's Namesake
        Model Young Man, A
        Mysterious Mr. Davey
        Never Again
        Pickles, Art and Sauerkraut
        Professional Scape Goat, The
        Professor's Romance, The
        Rainy, the Lion Killer
        Royal Wild West, The
        Too Many Husbands
        Who's Who in Hog's Hollow
        William Henry Jones' Courtship
1915   All for a Girl, aka All for the Love
        of a Girl
        Back to the Primitive
        Beautiful Thoughts
        Between the Two of Them
        Booble's Baby
        Case of Eugenics, A
        Combination, The
        Cub and the Daisy Chain, The
        Cupid's Column
        Deceivers, The
        Diplomatic Henry
        Following the Scent
        Fox Trot Finesse
        Hair of Her Head, The
        His Wife Knew About It
        Home Cure, The
        Homecoming of Henry, The
        Honeymoon Baby, The
        How John Came Home
        Is Christmas a Bore?
        Miss Sticky-Moufie-Kiss
        Mr. Brink of Bohemia
        Playing Dead
        Professional Diner, The
        Professor's Painless Cure, The
        Romantic Reggie
        Rooney's Sad Case
        Safe Investment, A
        Story of a Glove, The
        Their Agreement
        Their First Quarrel
        Timid Mr. Tootles, The

Unlucky Louey
Wanted, a Nurse
When Dumbleigh Saw the Joke
When Greek Meets Greek
When Two Play a Game

1916 At a Premium
At the Count of Ten
Borrowing Trouble
Childhood's Happy Days
Crosby's Rest Cure
Duplicity
Free Speech
Gravy
Help
Her Perfect Husband
His Rival
His Wife's Mother
It Never Got by
Jones' Auto, The
Lady in the Library, A
Nobody Home
Number One
One on Henry
Peace at Any Price
System Is Everything
Taking a Rest
Telegraphic Tangle, A
Their Divorce
Their First
Too Clever by Half

1917 As Other See Us
Awakening of Helene Minor, The
Blackmail
Caveman's Buff
Close Resemblance, A
Dentist, The
Handy Henry
Her Anniversaries
Her Economic Independence
Her First Game
Her Lesson
Her Obsession
High Cost of Living, The
His Curiosity
His Deadly Calm
His Double Life
His Ear for Music
His Perfect Day
Hist! Spies
Hypochondriacs
Joy of Freedom, The

Lest We Forget
Locked Out
Match Makers, The
Mr. Parker—Hero
Music Hath Charms
Nothing to Wear
One of the Finest
Patriot, The
Pest, The
Professional Patient, The
Putting It Over on Henry
Rebellion of Mr. Minor, The
Reliable Henry
Rubbing It In
Safety First
Shadowing Henry
Spirit of Merry Christmas, The
Too Much Henry
Tootsie
Twelve Good Hens and True
Unmarried Look, The
Wages No Object
Why They Left Home, aka Why
Henry Left Home

1918 After Henry
Before and After Taking
Bright Lights Dimmed, The
Financing the Fourth
Gas Logic
Help Wanted
His First Love
His Generosity
His Strength of Mind
Pay Day
Special Today
Their First Love
Their Mutual Motor
Under the Influence
When a Man's Married
Youthful Affair, A

1919 Amateur Liar, The
Harold, the Last of the Saxons
Romance and Rings
Squared

AS DIRECTOR

1911 Red Devils, The
1913 Beauty Unadorned
1914 Florida Enchantment, A
Horseshoe—For Luck
Innocent But Awkward

Jerry's Uncle's Namesake
Mysterious Mr. Davey
Never Again
Professional Scape Goat, The
Professor's Romance, The
Rainy, the Lion Killer
Royal Wild West, The
Stanley, the Lion-Killer
Too Many Husbands
William Henry Jones' Courtship

1915 All for a Girl, aka All for the Love
of a Girl
Back to the Primitive
Beautiful Thoughts
Between the Two of Them
Booble's Baby
Case of Eugenics, A
Combination, The
Cub and the Daisy Chain, The
Deceivers, The
Diplomatic Henry
Following the Scent
Fox Trot Finesse
Hair of Her Head, The
His Wife Knew About It
Home Cure, The
Honeymoon Baby, The
How John Came Home
Is Christmas a Bore?
Miss Sticky-Moufie-Kiss
Mr. Brink of Bohemia
Playing Dead
Professional Diner, The
Professor's Painless Cure, The
Romantic Reggie
Rooney's Sad Case
Safe Investment, A
Story of a Glove, The
Their Agreement
Their First Quarrel
Timid Mr. Tootles, The
Unlucky Louey
Wanted, a Nurse
When Dumbleigh Saw the Joke
When Greek Meets Greek
When Two Play a Game

1916 At a Premium
Between One and Two
Borrowing Trouble
Crosby's Rest Cure
Duplicity

Free Speech
Gravy
Help
Henry's Thanksgiving
Her Perfect Husband
His First Tooth
His Rival
His Wife's Mother
It Never Got by
Lady in the Library, A
Model Cook, The
Nobody Home
Number One
One on Henry
Peace at Any Price
Preparedness
Sweet Charity
Swooners, The
Symphony in Coal
Taking a Rest
Telegraphic Tangle, A
Their Divorce
Their First
Too Clever by Half

1917 *As Other See Us*
Awakening of Helene Minor, The
Blackmail
Caveman's Buff
Close Resemblance, A
Dentist, The
Handy Henry
Henry's Ancestors
Her Anniversaries
Her Economic Independence
Her First Game
Her Lesson
Her Obsession
High Cost of Living, The
His Curiosity
His Deadly Calm
His Double Life
His Ear for Music
His Little Spirit Girl
His Perfect Day
Hist! Spies
Joy of Freedom, The
Lest We Forget
Locked Out
Match Makers, The
Mr. Parker—Hero
Music Hath Charms

Nothing to Wear
Patriot, The
Professional Patient, The
Putting It Over on Henry
Rebellion of Mr. Minor, The
Reliable Henry
Rubbing It In
Safety First
Shadowing Henry
Spirit of Merry Christmas, The
Their Burglar
Too Much Henry
Tootsie
Twelve Good Hens and True
Unmarried Look, The
Wages No Object
Why They Left Home, aka *Why*
Henry Left Home

1918 *After Henry*
Before and After Taking
Bright Lights Dimmed, The
Gas Logic
Help Wanted
His First Love
His Generosity
His Strength of Mind
Pay Day
Special Today
Their Mutual Motor
Under the Influence
When a Man's Married
Youthful Affair, A

1919 *Amateur Liar, The*
Harold, the Last of the Saxons
Once a Mason
Romance and Rings
Squared

AS WRITER

1914 *Professional Scapegoat, The*
1915 *Combination, The*
Home Cure, The
Professional Diner, The
1917 *As Other See Us*
Close Resemblance, A
Dentist, The
Henry's Ancestors
Her Anniversaries
Her Economic Independence
Her Lesson
Her Obsession

His Curiosity
His Deadly Calm
His Ear for Music
Hist! Spies
Joy of Freedom, The
Lest We Forget
Match Makers, The
Mr. Parker—Hero
Music Hath Charms
Nothing to Wear
Patriot, The
Rebellion of Mr. Minor, The
Rubbing It In
Safety First
Shadowing Henry
Spirit of Merry Christmas, The
Their Burglar
Too Much Henry
Tootsie
Twelve Good Hens and True
Why They Left Home, aka *Why*
Henry Left Home

1918 *After Henry*
Before and After Taking
Bright Lights Dimmed, The
Gas Logic
His First Love
His Generosity
Pay Day
Special Today
Their Mutual Motor
Under the Influence
When a Man's Married
Youthful Affair, A

1919 *Amateur Liar, The*
Bunkered
Harold, the Last of the Saxons
Once a Mason
Squared

Bramwell Fletcher
(1904-1988)

AS ACTOR

1929 *To What Red Hell*
1930 *Raffles*
So This Is London
1931 *Daughter of the Dragon*
Men of the Sky
Millionaire, The

1932 *Once a lady*
Svengali
1932 *Bill of Divorcement, A*
Face on the Barroom Floor, The
Monkey's Paw, The
Mummy, The, aka *Cagliostro,* aka
Im-Ho-Tep, aka *King of the Dead*
Silent Witness
1933 *Only Yesterday*
Right to Romance, The
1934 *Nana* (uncredited)
Scarlet Pimpernel, The
1935 *Line Engaged*
1942 *Random Harvest*
Undying Monster, The
White Cargo
1943 *Immortal Sergeant*

Tom Green

(1971-   )

AS ACTOR

1998 *Clutch*
1998 *Chicken Tree, The*
1999 *Superstar*
1999 *Tom Green: Tonsil Hockey*
1999 *Tom Green: Something Smells
Funny*
2000 *Road Trip*
2000 *Charlie's Angels*
2001 *Freddy Got Fingered*
2002 *Say Uncle*

AS WRITER

2001 *Freddy Got Fingered*
1999 *Tom Green: Tonsil Hockey*

AS PRODUCER

1999 *Tom Green: Tonsil Hockey*

AS COMPOSER

1999 *Tom Green: Tonsil Hockey*

AS DIRECTOR

2001 *Freddy Got Fingered*

Robert Wilcox

(1910-1955)

AS ACTOR

1937 *Armored Car*
Carnival Queen
City Girl
Let Them Live
Man in Blue, The
Wild and Woolly
1938 *Gambling Ship*
Little Tough Guy
Rascals
Reckless Living
Swing That Cheer
Young Fugitives
1939 *Blondie Takes a Vacation*
Buried Alive
Kid From Texas, The
Man They Could Not Hang, The
Uncovered Doctor
1940 *Dreaming Out Loud*
Island of Doomed Men
Lone Wolf Strikes, The
Mysterious Doctor Satan
1946 *Unknown, The*

Wild Beauty
1947 *Vigilantes Return, The*
1966 *Dr. Satan's Robot* (TV)

Cara Williams

(1925-   )

AS ACTRESS

1943 *Happy Land*
1944 *In the Meantime, Darling*
Laura (uncredited)
Something for the Boys
Sweet and Lowdown
1945 *Don Juan Quilligan*
Spider, The
1947 *Boomerang!*
1948 *Saxon Charm, The*
Sitting Pretty
1949 *Knock on Any door*
1951 *Monte Carlo Baby*
1953 *Girl Next Door, The*
Great Diamond Robbery, The
1956 *Meet Me in Las Vegas,* aka *Viva
Las Vegas!*
1957 *Helen Morgan Story, The,* aka
Why Was I Born?
1958 *Defiant Ones, The*
1959 *Never Steal Anything Small*
1963 *Man from the Diner's Club, The*
1971 *Doctors' Wives*
1977 *White Buffalo, The,* aka *Hunt to
Kill*
1978 *One Man Jury,* aka *Dead on
Arrival*

Bibliography

NOTE: *Unless indicated otherwise, quotes by Louisa Lane Drew, John Drew, and Lionel, Ethel, John, Diana, and Drew Barrymore were drawn from their autobiographies.*

Alpert, Hollis. *The Barrymores*. New York: Dial Press, 1964.

The American Stage of Today: Biographies and Photographs of One Hundred Leading Actors and Actresses. New York: P.F. Collier & Son, 1909.

Barnes, Eric Wollencott. *The Man Who Lived Twice: The Biography of Edward Sheldon*. New York: Charles Scribner's Sons, 1956.

Barrymore, Diana, and Gerald Frank. *Too Much, Too Soon*. New York: Holt, 1957.

Barrymore, Drew, with Todd Gold. *Little Lost Girl*. New York: Pocket, 1991.

Barrymore, Elaine, and Sanford Dody. *All My Sins Remembered*. New York: Appleton-Century, 1964.

Barrymore, Ethel. *Memories: An Autobiography*. New York: Harper, 1955.

Barrymore, John. *Confessions of an Actor*. New York: Curtis, 1925.

Barrymore, John. *We Three*. New York: Saalfield, 1935.

Barrymore, Lionel, as told to Cameron Shipp. *We Barrymores*. New York: Appleton-Century-Crofts, 1951.

Barrymore, Maurice H. *Najezda*. London: Lord Chamberlain's Office, 1885.

Behlmer, Rudy. *Inside Warner Bros. (1935-1951)*. New York: Simon and Schuster, 1985.

Biery, Ruth. "The Lion Tamer of 'Grand Hotel.'" *Photoplay Magazine*, July 1932.

"Birds of the Islands off the Coast of Southern California," by Alfred Brazier Howell, Cooper Ornithological Club, Pacific Coast Avifauna, Number 12. Hollywood California, Published by The Club, June 30, 1917.

"British Sea Angler's Society's Quarterly," December 1930, Vol. XXIII-No. 94. London. (written in John Barrymore's hand, "Bob - ox2805," on cover-csh).

Carroll, David. *The Matinee Idols*. New York: Galahad, 1972.

Chicago Academy of Sciences, Vol. I, Art IX, 1869 (Mr. J.A. Allen with sincere regards of W.H. Dall) (Art. IX List of the Birds of Alaska, with Bibliographical Notes by Wm. H. Dall and H.M. Bannister).

Conrad, Earl. *Errol Flynn: A Memoir*. New York: Dodd, Mead, 1978.

Costello, Helene. "The Fabulous Costellos." *American Weekly*, Oct. 10, 1948, 6-7.

Costello, Maurice. "What It Meant to Be a Star in 1911." *Motion Picture*, 1941.

Davies, Marion. *The Times We Had*. New York: Ballantine Books, 1977.

"Descriptions of Apparently New South American Birds, with Notes on Some Little Known Species," by Charles B. Cory, Curator of Department of Zoology. Field Museum of Natural History, Publication 190. Ornithological Series, Vol. 1, No. 10. Chicago, U.S.A., August 30, 1916.

"Descriptions of New Birds from South America and Adjacent Islands," by Charles B. Cory, Curator of Department of Zoology, Field of Natural History, Publication 18, Ornithological Series, Vol. 1, No. 8, Chicago, U.S.A., February 23, 1915.

Dick, Bernard. *City of Dreams: The Making and Remaking of Universal Pictures*. Lexington: Univ. Press of Kentucky, 1997.

Drew, John. *My Years on the Stage*. New York: Dutton, 1922.

Drew, Mrs. John [Louisa Lane]. *Autobiographical Sketch of Mrs. John Drew*. New York: Charles Scribner's Sons, 1899.

Esquire, the Magazine for Men, December, 1959, "The Dark World of John Barrymore" (two pages of John Barrymore's artwork-csh) p. 220-221.

Eyman, Scott. *The Speed of Sound: Hollywood and the Talkie Revolution, 1926-1930*. New York: Simon and Schuster, 1997.

Fowler, Gene. *Good Night, Sweet Prince: The Life and Times of John Barrymore*. New York: Viking, 1943.

Fowler, Gene. *Minutes of the Last Meeting*. New York: Viking, 1954.

Fowler, Will. *"Reporters": Memoirs of a Young Newspaperman*. Malibu: Roundtable, 1991.

Fowler, Will. *The Young Man from Denver*. Garden City: Doubleday, 1962.

Furman, Leah & Elina. *Happily Ever After: The Drew Barrymore Story*. New York: Ballantine, 2000.

Glazer, Barney. Radio interview with Maurice Costello. 1936.

Griffith, Richard. *The Movie Stars*. Garden City: Doubleday, 1970.

Hays, Will H. *The Memoirs of Will H. Hays*. Garden City: Doubleday, 1955.

Heide, Robert, and John Gilman. *Starstruck: The Wonderful World of Movie Memorabilia*. Garden City: Doubleday: 1986.

Kanin, Garson. *Hollywood: Stars and Starlets, Tycoons and Flesh-Peddlers, Moviemakers and Moneymakers, Frauds and Geniuses, Hopefuls and Has-Beens, Great Lovers and Sex Symbols*. New York: Viking, 1967.

Koblar, John. *Damned in Paradise: The Life of John Barrymore*. New York: Antheneum, 1977.

Kotsilibas-Davis, James. *The Barrymores: The Royal Family in Hollywood*. New York: Crown, 1981.

Kotsilibas-Davis, James. *Good Times, Great Times: The Odyssey of Maurice Barrymore*. Garden City: Doubleday, 1977.

LeBrun, George P., as told to Edward D. Radin. *It's Time to Tell*. New York: William Morrow, 1962.

Lee, Betty. *Marie Dressler: The Unlikeliest Star*. Lexington: Univ. Press of Kentucky, 1997.

Lennig, Arthur. *Stroheim*. Lexington: Univ. Press of Kentucky, 2000.

Marcosson, Isaac F., and Daniel Frohman. *Charles Frohman: Manager and Man*. New York: Harper & Brothers, 1916.

Meaker, M.J. "You'll See, Mr. Atkinson." In *Sudden Endings*, ed. M.J. Meaker. Garden City: Doubleday, 1964. 168-188.

Meredith, Burgess. *So Far, So Good: A Memoir*. New York: Little, Brown, 1994.

Modern Screen Magazine p. 13-Welcome Back Dolores, [.30_I Choose John Barrymore, p. 52-The Infanta, p. 37-Maurice Costello c. 1930-31

Mordden, Ethan. *The Hollywood Studios: House Style in the Golden Age of the Movies*. New York: Knopf, 1988.

Mordden, Ethan. *Movie Star: A Look at the Women Who Made Hollywood*. New York: St. Martin's, 1983.

Naabe, Derek. *Philadelphia's Theater Heritage*. Pennsylvania Historical Society, n.d.

"Notes on South American Birds, with descriptions of New Species," by Charles B. Cory, Curator of Department of Zoology. Field Museum of Natural History, Publication 183, Ornithological Series, Vol. 1, No. 9; Chicago, U.S.A., August 7, 1915.

Peters, Margot. *The House of Barrymore*. New York: Knopf, 1990.

Power-Waters, Alma. *John Barrymore: The Legend and the Man*. New York: Julien Messner, 1948.

Quinn, Anthony, with Daniel Paisner. *One Man Tango*. New York: HarperCollins, 1995.

Ramsaye, Terry. *A Million and One Nights: A History of the Motion Picture Through 1925*. New York: Simon and Schuster, 1964.

Sarris, Andrew. *"You Ain't Heard Nothin' Yet": The American Talking Film, History and Memory, 1927-1949*.

Sennett, Ted. *Warner Brothers Presents: The Most Exciting Years—from the* Jazz Singer *to* White Heat. N.p.: Arlington House, 1971.

Skal, David J., and Elias Savada. *Dark Carnival: The Secret World of Tod Browning, Hollywood's Master of the Macabre*. New York: Anchor, 1995.

Stein, Charles W., ed. *American Vaudeville as Seen by Its Contemporaries*. New York: Knopf, 1984.

Sherman, Vincent. *Studio Affairs: My Life as a Film Director*. Lexington: Univ. of Kentucky Press, 1996.

Talmage, Norma. "Close ups." *Saturday Evening Post*, March 12, 1927.

Teichmann, Howard. *George S. Kaufman: An Intimate Portrait*. New York: Antheneum, 1972.

Thomas, Bob. *Joan Crawford: A Biography*. New York: Simon and Schuster, 1978.

Thomson, David. *Rosebud: The Story of Orson Welles*. New York: Knopf, 1996.

Troyan, Michael. *A Rose for Mrs. Miniver: The Life of Greer Garson*. Lexington: Univ. Press of Kentucky, 1999.

Wallace, Irving. *The Fabulous Showman: The Life and Times of P.T. Barnum*. New York: Knopf, 1959.

Whitfield, Eileen. *Pickford: The Woman Who Made Hollywood*. Lexington: Univ. press of Kentucky, 1997.

Wiles, Buster, with William Donati. *My Days with Errol Flynn: The Autobiography of Stuntman Buster Wiles*. Santa Monica: Roundtable, 1988.

Winter, William. "Foreword." In *The American Stage of Today: Biographies and Photographs of One Hundred Leading Actors and Actresses*. New York: P.F. Collier & Son, 1909.

"Zoologica, Studies of a Tropical Jungle at Kartabo, British Guiana," by William Beebe, Scientific Contributions of the New York Zoological Society, Department of Tropical Research, Kartabo, British Guiana, Vol. VI, No. 1. March 11, 1925, Published by the Society of the Zoological Park, New York.

Personal Diaries and Letters of John Barrymore, Dolores Costello, Helene Costello, Maurice Costello, Mae Costello.

Contributors

John Drew Barrymore is the instigator of this book, and he approved its final form. He, of course, furnished most of the "Barrymorebelia," and it was his fond wish that the writing herein would depict his celebrated relatives with respect.

Ralph Anthony Lumi, long time personal friend of John Drew Barrymore, has been the mainstay and guiding light of this endeavor, believing in its value and encouraging John to assist in its completion. His creative ideas are the foundation of the book, and he has read, reread, edited, and critiqued over these twenty years of the project.

Carol Stein Hoffman, the writer, holds a master's degree in Clinical Art Psychotherapy from Immaculate Heart College and Cedars-Sinai Mental Hospital Clinic (Thalians), Los Angeles, California, and has studied sculpture at California State University, Northridge. She holds a bachelor's degree in Art and Art History from the University of Wisconsin, and she attended Albright Art School at the University of Buffalo and the University of Pennsylvania, where she studied Art History. She studied at the Summer Academy of Art, Salzburg, Austria, under the master Oscar Kokoshka, expressionist artist and playwright.

Index

NOTE: *Italic page numbers indicate photographs.*